The Jesuits in the United States

The Jesuits
in the
United States

A Concise History

DAVID J. COLLINS

GEORGETOWN UNIVERSITY PRESS / WASHINGTON, DC

The publisher is not responsible for third-party websites or their content. URL links were active at time of publication.

Cataloging-in-Publication data is on file with the Library of Congress.

ISBN 978-1-64712-348-2 (hardcover)
ISBN 978-1-64712-349-9 (ebook)

♾ This paper meets the requirements of ANSI/NISO Z39.48-1992 (Permanence of Paper).

24 23   9 8 7 6 5 4 3 2 First printing
Printed in the United States of America

Cover design by Nathan Putens
Interior design by Faye Thaxton, Classic City Composition

CONTENTS

FIGURES

PREFACE

The founder of the Jesuit order, Saint Ignatius Loyola, wrote into the *Constitutions*, its primary governing document, "Our vocation is to travel through the world and to live in any part of it where there is hope of greater service to God and of help of souls." One corner of the world where its members have traveled, lived, and aspired to these lofty goals for nearly five centuries and to the present day is North America. This book is about those Jesuits.

Though *about* Jesuits, this is a book *for* all kinds of people. It is a book for people who have heard something about Jesuits—good, bad, or neutral—but are not sure exactly what a Jesuit is. It is a book for those who know a Jesuit or of a Jesuit and want to know more about the organization of which he is a part and to which he has dedicated his life. It is a look at the Jesuits for folks who think that history can offer insights into the present. Those readers and aims are what inspired this book, which started as notes for an introductory workshop for people who knew something about contemporary Jesuits but wanted to understand them better through their history. This book does not tell the whole history of the Society of Jesus (as the Jesuit organization is formally named), but focuses on the Jesuits active in the United States. Along these lines, the book will also be of interest to those who have no immediate curiosity about Jesuits but are curious about religion in America. On this point I am reminded of something a professor of religious history told a group of us undergraduates in his class on American Catholicism forty years ago: "The history of America cannot be told without the history of religion, the history of American religion cannot be told without the history of Catholicism, and the history of Catholicism in America cannot be told without the history of Jesuits in America." And so, this book.

Before I offer an introduction, chapter by chapter, of this book, I need to alert the reader to a couple of challenges I faced as I wrote. The reader may have noticed a hint of the first challenge in the differences between the book's title and its topic as expressed in the last paragraph. The former speaks of Jesuits *in the United States*; the latter, of Jesuits *in America*. These terms are of course not identical—the United States is but one part even of *North* America. Furthermore, the national history of the United States is only half the nearly five centuries that this book covers. Maybe the problem could be dismissed as a technicality. But hidden in the incongruities is actually something quite noteworthy: centuries before the United States came into existence, extensive Jesuit activity was under way in the Americas, and this activity in the colonial period laid important groundwork for the order's later activity in the United States proper.

On top of that, no Jesuit regional history ever unfolds in isolation from the rest of Jesuit history. Ever since Francis Xavier (1506–52) departed Lisbon for Goa in 1541, Jesuit activity has been global. The history of Jesuits in America is part of this global activity, and there have been geopolitical dimensions to the history from the beginning. Jesuits started arriving in the Americas in the sixteenth century only at the indulgence of Europe's colonizing crowned heads. The Jesuits who served in these colonies came from across Europe. Because the colonialized territories in those times do not match up with national boundaries today, in the earlier chapters we keep in our field of view mainly the North American continent north and east of the Rio Grande. In later chapters, we narrow the focus to Jesuits in the United States itself. But even then, nineteenth-century French missions extending down from Canada and up from New Orleans, recurrent waves of refugee Jesuits from various parts of Europe, a porous frontier

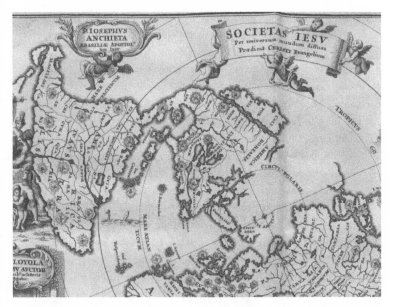

FIGURE 1 "The Society of Jesus, spread across the whole world, preaches the gospel of Christ" (detail), from Henrich Scherer's *Geographia hierarchica* (Munich, 1703). The Americas are in the upper left of this global map's polar projection. The IHS emblems mark Jesuit settlements worldwide, for example, in La Florida, New France, Virginia (for Maryland), and "the lands of the Huron and Iroquois" (on the Great Lakes). Scherer (1628–1704) was an instructor at the Jesuit college in Dillingen in Germany and the tutor to royal princes in Munich. The atlas was his life's work, drafted from Jesuit reports from around the globe. Despite some geographical inaccuracies—for example, the European misperception of Baja California as an island rather than a peninsula—the atlas reflects the day's most advanced cartographical techniques, and the polar projection itself was highly innovative. Source: "Societas Iesu, per universum mundum diffusa predicat christi evangelium," in *Geographia hierarchica*, by Heinrich Scherer (Munich, 1703), fol. III. Bayerische Staatsbibliothek, Munich, Res/4 Geo.u. 99 a-2.

between the Jesuit United States and Jesuit Canada, and the presence of US Jesuits in foreign missionary territories in the twentieth century always make the history more than just a national one. What at first glance seems an inconvenience of language—how to identify the geographical and chronological scope of this volume—in fact sets the stage for a transnational history in a country that itself is a singularly diverse, modern multiculture.

The range of Jesuit activities is at the heart of the second challenge: over those four and a half centuries, the variety has been extraordinary, and the Jesuits themselves comprise a rich, colorful assortment of talents and temperaments. Furthermore, there has been little that the Jesuits have succeeded or failed at on their own. Colleagues and coworkers, donors and patrons, students and alumni, parishioners, fellow religious (women and men), priests and bishops, state legislatures and tribal councils, legislators and chiefs, tenant farmers and enslaved people—the list goes on and on—all made the Jesuit history possible. The challenge in a book like this is to form into an intelligible storyline a complex regional history that captures as much as possible of the who, the what, the how, and the why of this massive Jesuit enterprise. And, yes, as a "concise history," in under fifty thousand words!

To achieve these goals, the book pays closest attention to the Jesuits themselves, as individuals and a group. Institutions, like schools, and organizational structures, like missions, are favored in this volume for several reasons—among them, because sources are accessible and abundant; because so many Jesuits can be accounted for in this way; and because so many other people are at least implicitly included, especially through educational institutions.

In the end, this book does not aspire to be the definitive history of the Jesuits in the United States but rather to whet the readers' appetite for more. By way of satisfying this appetite, there are suggestions for further reading at the end of each chapter. These suggestions constitute much of what I drew from in composing this volume. Some references point the reader to historical documents; others note the works of historians in their areas of expertise. These readings vary in level of technicality; some are more academic, and some are more popular. Hopefully, there is something for everyone in these lists.

ACKNOWLEDGMENTS

Before we begin, a quick and happy detour: I wish to thank those who helped and encouraged this project. Before its contents were imagined as composing a book, they had the form of a week-long seminar for the Jesuit novices of the United States and Canada. I am grateful to the novice directors and their assistants—especially Father James Carr, Father Mark Thibodeaux, and Father Charlie Rodrigues—for inviting me to participate in their biennial, month-long history workshop in Denver from 2013 to 2017. I am grateful also to the novices themselves, whose engagement with the materials was energetic and whose questions and reactions served, in effect, as a first round of editing for what readers now hold in their hands. I wish to thank as well Father Pierre Sauvage for inviting me in 2015 to turn the seminars and lectures into a book for his series, *La petite bibliothèque Jésuite*; Kari Nelson, who as an undergraduate at Georgetown University aided my research in 2016; the historians Gerald Fogarty, Thomas McCoog, and John O'Malley (†2022), as well as the anonymous readers provided by the press, for reading and commenting on the entire volume in draft; Seth Meehan of the Institute for Advanced Jesuit Studies at Boston College, for help with chapter 3; and Christopher Gurley, for help on aspects of African American Catholicism, especially in chapter 4. Katherine Collins and a selected group of readers from her parish, Kevin Sullivan, and Madeline Vitek likewise read and commented on the entire manuscript to help clarify the language and highlight key themes. Ed Beckett, Michael Buckley (†2019),

Matt Carnes, Drew Christiansen (†2022), Vince Conti, Tim O'Brien, Bill Ryan, and Chris Steck were helpful interlocutors as I worked on chapter 5 and the epilogue, even though (or, perhaps, especially because) there was not agreement on all interpretive points among us. The staffs of the Booth Family Center for Special Collections at Georgetown University, especially Keith Gorman, and of the Jesuit Archives and Research Center in Saint Louis, especially David Miros, Daniel Peterson at Santa Clara University, and Amy Page at Marquette University, were helpful during research and in the selection of illustrations. While responsibility for the book's flaws lies with me, these and other friends and colleagues have made the volume immeasurably better than it would have been without them.

And finally, with gratitude, I dedicate this book to the Southern Maryland parishes of Saint Peter Claver in Ridge, Saint Francis Xavier in Newtowne, and Saint Ignatius Loyola at Chapel Point, which for many generations have welcomed Jesuits and remind me again and again that God's grace is as powerful in the present as it ever was in the past.

David J. Collins, SJ
Washington, DC
November 23, 2022

Introduction:
Laying Foundations

THIS BOOK IS DIVIDED into five chapters. Though the chapters are arranged chronologically, there is always some "spillage" forward or backward because trends in Jesuit history, as in all history, rarely reach moments of absolute transition or culmination. Usually what binds each chapter is some distinctive intersection of what the Jesuits were doing, what American Catholics looked like, and where Catholics fit in larger US society.

The particulars of these three components were (and are) always shifting. Two threads run through the whole history—sometimes intersecting, always changing relative to each other, and never completely isolated from each other. The first one has to do with Jesuit contact and work with Native Americans; the second, with European settlers, immigrants, and these legacy populations to the present day. That at the end of the twentieth century activities connected to the former are so diminished by many measures—number of mission stations, amount of dedicated manpower, and so on—and in comparison with any earlier point in Jesuit history, should not distract the reader from the enormous significance of that work for the Jesuits throughout their history in upper North America. The possibilities associated with the Indigenous populations attracted hundreds of European Jesuits to the Americas and still today inspire the life work of many Jesuits. This history was complicated as it played out and is complicated as it is looked back on today, ever more so in the present moment. As this book goes to press, the history of settlers' treatment of Native peoples is coming under new scrutiny. That is a good thing. It will mean that the assessment of Jesuit cooperation with colonial, state, and national governments in their treatment of Native peoples will change, as also the Church's pursuit of its "Great Commission" to "make disciples of and baptize all nations." This book tries to capture the current state of scholarship, but the reader should be alerted to how quickly it is changing.

The other thread, the one having to do with the "settler" population and its "descendants," is this: the Jesuits have been committed to the ideal that Catholics could make a home in, be integrated in, thrive in, and productively shape mainstream American society. This ideal can be contrasted to an alternate ideal that looks to the creation of a Catholic community situated in but insulated from the greater American society. Both modes of being American have been prominent ways of pursuing the American Dream. Indeed, a spectrum can be drawn that places the American "melting pot" achieved by a strategy of "mainstreaming" at one end and the American "salad bowl" achieved by a strategy of "ghettoizing" at the other. How mainstreaming and ghettoizing happen along these lines to any one group has as much to do with forces internal to a community as external to it; and self-segregation and imposed segregation reinforce each other, community by community, in an infinite range of ways. To offer two quite different examples of isolating communities: think of the Old Order Amish in Ohio and Pennsylvania and of twentieth-century gay communities in the Castro district and Greenwich Village. Though many people throughout history have preferred (and do prefer) the ghettoized model for Catholicism, some of them Catholics themselves, the Jesuits' contribution to Catholicism in America has been decidedly on the mainstreaming side of the spectrum.

We will return to such overarching themes in the epilogue. In the meantime, we must start with a story that begins in 1566. In chapter 1, we explore Jesuit activities in colonial North America, which piggybacked on three European colonizing powers—the Spanish, the French, and the English—in their attempts to establish a foothold in North America. Each had failures before it had successes, and only the latter two succeeded on the North Atlantic coast. Spanish Jesuits ultimately reoriented themselves from Florida to Mexico. French Jesuits, after several failed attempts at the beginning of the sixteenth century, finally in the 1630s got a foothold in Quebec City from which to launch their work throughout New France. Unlike in New Spain and New France, in the English colony of Maryland, Catholics were a small minority of colonists but were among the social elite. This was an odd situation. In England and its colonies, legal prejudice against and social hostility toward Catholicism were a serious threat, which in Maryland waxed and waned until Independence. Jesuits arrived with the Catholics at the invitation of the Catholic proprietor in 1634. The history of these colonial Jesuits is a history of how they and the small Catholic community to which they ministered negotiated this unusual and unstable situation.

Chapter 2 explores what happened when the papacy first dissolved and then restored the order. The reasons for the Suppression are complex and beyond the scope and capacity of this small volume. A thumbnail sketch would begin with one pope's letter in 1773 that suppressed the order and a later pope's decree that restored it in 1814. When we look more closely, however, we see that the story is not nearly so simple and is much more interesting. On one hand, royal suppressions in Spain and France anticipated the papal one. On the other hand, a small remnant of Jesuits remained active in Russia, where Empress Catherine the Great prohibited the implementation of the original papal letter. Furthermore, while the Catholic hierarchy enforced the Suppression in the English colonies, its effects were different from those anywhere else in the world, both for the suddenly former Jesuits and for the Church. In 1773 the only priests in the Thirteen Colonies were Jesuits, and there had never been a local bishop to guide the Church, only the order's religious superiors. What emerged from this disorder was remarkable: a national Church, with a bishop (eventually) and local clergy who were not Jesuits (though many had been). By the time the Society was restored in the United States, there was a small but vibrant Church at last in place. The Jesuits would become a crucial part of this, but the order was no longer the driving force behind it, as it had been before. One twist in the remarkable story is that the Suppression ended in the United States not with the papal bull of 1814 but nearly a decade earlier with the affiliation of a few former Jesuits with the order's remnant in Russia. Like so much else that is re-counted in this chapter, this restoration was due to the tireless efforts and patient diplomacy of the nation's first bishop, John Carroll, himself a former Jesuit. This chapter also devotes itself to a sketch of the sad history of Jesuit slaveholding: enslaved people were a kind of property the Jesuits claimed in the colonial period, lost at the Suppression, fought to regain with the Restoration, and benefited from until the end of the Civil War.

The nineteenth century, taken as a whole, was a period of great expansion for the Jesuits, the Church, and the country as a whole. For the Jesuits, as for the nation, the growth in membership had a lot to do with immigration. Because of aggressive anticlerical laws and revolutions at home, hundreds of European Jesuits arrived in the nineteenth century as refugees, and some European provinces made commitments to relocate to the United States. These Jesuits tended also to arrive in waves by nation of origin and then to settle in and take responsibility over specific regions of the United States and its western territories. Chapter 3 follows these waves and concentrates, in turn, on the Belgian Jesuits, as they landed in Saint Louis and spread across the Midwest and Great Plains; the Italians, as the moved to the Rockies, into the Pacific North-west, and into California; the French, as they returned to a corri-dor stretching from Quebec to New Orleans and expanded into New York; and the Germans, as they spread across the Great Lakes region and worked their way into the Indian territory of the Great Plains. Sometimes it looks as if these emergent missions maintained stronger relations with their home provinces than with their Jesuit neighbors in North America. But much of what they were actually doing was quite similar: these were brick-and-mortar years for the Church as a whole and for the Jesuits in particular, who, often at the invitation of local bishops, arrived in new cities and established a full range of works centered on a school and a parish. Similar strategies were being followed in their missions to the Native Americans. These common works and the inevitable exchange of personnel encouraged networks across these ethnic and geographical divides. The clearest signal of this integration came in the opening years of the next century, when Rome uncoupled these provinces and missions from their European "mother" provinces and linked them administratively to one another to encourage yet more cooperation and coordination in the efforts already happening across the United States.

As the Church continued to grow in the early twentieth century, the significance of the new waves of Catholic immigrants was matched by the increasing size of Catholic families with several generations already in the country. A notable demographic shift within the Jesuits followed this development: the flow of refugee personnel waned but was more than made up for in home-grown recruits. Here is where chapter 4 begins. The Jesuits continued developing the infrastructure they had begun in the previous century, especially the schools, and developed new ministries in the service of a Catholic population that was a substantial and growing proportion of American labor and also making inroads into business. National and international worries over communism drove Jesuit outreach to both groups, and their strategy attempted to encompass both popular and scholarly modes of addressing what was known as "the social question." Under the direction of the Chicago-born Jesuit Daniel Lord, the Sodality of Our Lady, whose origins echoed the earliest efforts of the order at the Catholic renewal in sixteenth-century Europe, annually gathered hundreds of thousands of Catholic young people to encourage a new Catholic activism in the American public sphere. Simultaneously, the order was founding think tanks and policy institutes, the so-called Institutes of Social Order, and committing younger Jesuits to the advanced study of the social sciences as well. Both the Church and the order were coming into their own in a country that viewed Catholicism skeptically but that was coming to see the Church's growth as contributing to the nation's own best interests.

Chapter 5 attempts to capture the late-twentieth-century history of the order by highlighting two very different sets of forces shaping Church and society, sometimes in coordination, sometimes at cross purposes. The first set is the theological ideals that came to powerful expression at the Second Vatican Council (1961–64) and for the Jesuits in particular in a pair of general congregations (its highest governing body) that took place in 1964–65 and 1974–75. The second set comprises social forces moving believers and unbelievers alike toward greater senses of autonomy from and skepticism toward religion and other traditional authority. Two factors consequently dominated Jesuit life and work: a renewal of their spirituality, and a diminishment in their numbers. These factors, more than any others in this period, shaped how Jesuits thought about themselves and how they—sometimes inspired by new ideals, sometimes forced out of necessity by their shrinking membership—related to their works and institutions, the laity and the hierarchy, and broader society.

These factors continue to do so, making conclusions all the more difficult to draw. Many significant events could be pointed to as marking the beginning of the twenty-first century in important ways for the US Jesuits. None of them seems adequate, even that most remarkable of them, the election of a South American Jesuit as pope. Nonetheless, the epilogue provides the opportunity to consider the strongest threads to be found in the preceding five chapters and to speculate about how these may be found in the present and hint at a future. In the final analysis, such ruminations belong not to historians but to their readers.

1

Colonies, 1566–1773

———◆◆◆———

JESUITS HAVE BEEN ACTIVE in upper North America—the territory roughly corresponding to today's United States and Canada—since the mid–sixteenth century. For the first three quarters of this history, their activity was largely a European enterprise. Most Jesuits were European born, and most people they served, even given the attraction of and commitment to the Native American missions, were of European origin and descent. A vexing question throughout this period was what it meant to become American and how that should shape what the Jesuits should do, whether working in a burgeoning port town with European immigrants or in the Rocky Mountains with Native Americans. In these respects, the story of the Jesuits in the United States is a classically American one, which starts with the colonial powers that brought the Jesuits to the Americas in the first place. The three colonizing empires critical to the early history of the Jesuits are the Spanish, the French, and the British. With them we begin.

NEW SPAIN

Nearly a half century before English or French Jesuits ever found a foothold in upper North America, Jesuits in concert with the Spanish Crown were making modest, short-lived efforts at

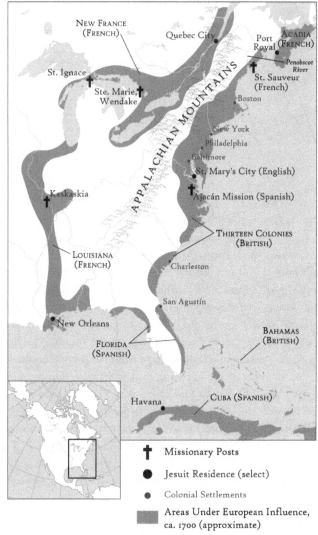

FIGURE 1.1 Map of North America's East Coast from Havana to the Gulf of Saint Lawrence and inland to the Mississippi River, highlighting selected Jesuit settlements in the colonial period. Source: Map of Jesuit settlements in eastern North America, by Geoffrey Wallace, for this volume.

establishing a mission on the North American Atlantic Coast. Pedro Menéndez de Avilés, the explorer who founded San Agustín (Saint Augustine) in La Florida, invited Jesuits to come and Christianize the Native peoples there in 1566. At the time, La Florida constituted a vice province of the Jesuit province of Peru. Because of perceived royal ambivalence to expansion in La Florida, the mission superior, Juan Bautista de Segura (c. 1530–71—*note that these birth and death dates in parentheses at a person's first mention indicate membership in the Jesuit order; the initials "SJ" are generally not appended to the name; "left" indicates the year of canonical separation from the Society, whether voluntary or involuntary*), decided to suppress the mission in San Agustín and return the bulk of the community to Havana but also to explore possibilities to the north himself with several companions. That contingent traveled up the coast as far as the Bahía de Madre de Dios (the Chesapeake Bay) and attempted to found a mission, the Ajacán, in September 1570 somewhere near the mouth of what the English later named the York River. Five months later, a lone survivor returned to San Agustín telling of an assault by Native people that put an end not just to the fledgling mission but to Jesuit efforts in La Florida and to the north altogether. The remaining Jesuits in Havana wrote to the head of the order in Rome, Francis Borgia (1510–72), advising that men be sent elsewhere.

Borgia received that caution simultaneously with a new request from the king of Spain: Philip II wanted Jesuits in Mexico. By 1571 Philip's authority extended over Spain, and its new world empire, as well as over Naples, Sicily, and the Netherlands. He was keenly interested in the activities of the Church throughout his realm, and his ecclesiastical involvement ranged from the generous endowments of churches and religious houses to intrusive interventions into parish and monastic life. Concerned for maintaining both religious orthodoxy and loyalty to the Crown, Philip superintended the assignment of Spanish priests outside Spain and of foreign priests to the colonial missions. The king's sudden interest in recruiting Jesuits to Mexico not only corresponded to the Jesuits' new missionary verve but, given the order's dependence

P.Ludovicus Qviros Gabriel, de Solis et Ioannes Mendez S. J. Hispani
in Florida pro Christi fide barbare enecti. A. 1571 ✝ February.
C.Screta del.

FIGURE 1.2 "Martyrdom of Luis de Quirós and companions, 1571,"
from Matthius Tanner's *Societas Jesu usque ad sanguinis et vitae profusionem militans* (Prague, 1675). Some nineteen Jesuits were killed in the
colonial period within the present limits of the United States, two by the
English, and others by Native Americans. The earliest was Pedro Martinez,
a Spaniard working with Indigenous peoples outside San Agustín, in 1566;
the last was Claude Virot, a Frenchman who was serving as an army chaplain in Genesee Valley, New York, in 1759. Whatever the motives behind
their killings, the martyrs' imputed heroism and innocence inspired new re-

on princely cooperation for its initiatives whether at home and abroad, was also the kind of offer they could not refuse.

The Mexico mission quickly proved itself exactly as the mission in Florida had not, a success: Jesuits arrived in Mexico City on September 28, 1572. From this staging point, the Jesuit mission expanded steadily into upper North America. In the mid–eighteenth century the mission in the Sonoran Desert, an area that now straddles the US–Mexican frontier, included over thirty churches and encompassed nearly one hundred villages. The mission's purpose was the evangelization of local peoples and their protection from the crassest forms of Spanish exploitation, even as it led ineluctably to their submission to colonial control. The Crown's expulsion of the Jesuits from New Spain in 1767 terminated their mission activities there. The Franciscan friars took over existing missions in the Sonoran Desert. The expulsion also ended ambitious Jesuit plans to expand from Baja into Alta California. The Dominican friars were assigned the Jesuit establishments in Baja California, and the Franciscans stepped in to found twenty-one missions between 1769 and 1823, from San Diego to Sonoma. When a century later the Jesuits returned to the region, European immigrant and Hispanic populations in cities were the focus of their attention rather than Native ones. In short, the colonial Spanish mission to Native populations in the

cruits and resources for the missions. In his lavishly illustrated seventeenth-century necrology of Jesuit martyrs worldwide, Tanner (1630–92), the sometime Jesuit rector of the Charles University in Prague, devoted many pages and seven images to the missions of La Florida and New France. The illustrations reflect typical tendencies to barbarize the Native Americans, insinuating their need not only for Christianization but also civilization (note in this illustration that the Jesuits are shown shot in the back). This engraving marks the death of five Jesuits, including two baptized natives who had taken vows in Havana, at the Ajacán mission near the mouth of the Chesapeake Bay, on February 8, 1571. Source: "Martyrdom of Luis de Quirós and companions, 1571," in *Societas Jesu usque ad sanguinis et vitae profusionem militans*, by Matthius Tanner (Prague, 1675), p. 448. Georgetown University, Washington, Booth Family Center for Special Collections (hereafter BFCSC), GTC Z991.

American southwest flourished as long as it lasted, was handed over to others by necessity, and was not returned to when the (Italian) Jesuits returned to the region a century later.

NEW FRANCE

A second effort at settling on the North American East Coast began in 1611, when Jesuits landed at Penobscot Bay, then in New France and now in Maine. The French efforts began with little more success than the earlier Spanish efforts in La Florida. The French Jesuits shared the Spaniards' earlier goal of evangelizing Indigenous peoples, but sustained contact proved elusive. Disputes between the colonial proprietor and the missioners, the mistrust of French Calvinists, and the hostility of English Puritans in the Massachusetts Bay Colony and even Anglicans in Virginia hobbled the earliest Jesuit ventures in and around Port Royal and along the Penobscot River in Acadia, from which Jesuits withdrew in 1613. Jesuits initiated a second effort in 1625 in Quebec, when the city's population was still under 100, but English raiding parties upended this effort by occupying the city in 1629. The Jesuits first gained long-term traction in 1634 with the foundations of a college in Quebec and a mission in Huronia to the west.

The arrivals in this period included some of the most talented and determined Jesuits of the era: Ennemond Massé (1575–1646), Charles Lalement (1587–1674), Paul le Jeune (1591–1664), and Jean de Brébeuf (1593–1649). Le Jeune's route to the new world is illustrative of the varied ways French Jesuits arrived in the colonies. He converted from Calvinism to Catholicism at age sixteen, entered the Society five years later, and was inspired by Massé's accounts of the failed Port Royal mission to petition his superiors for an assignment there. He taught several years at the Jesuits' colleges in Rennes and Bourges before his ordination, and then as a priest he taught Rhetoric at the colleges in Nevers and Caen and served as a preacher in Dieppe, before at last receiving his desired assignment to New France in 1632. In 1649 he returned to France, where his efforts on behalf of the mission as its procurator (principal fund-raiser), it could be said, were even more fruitful than his work in the mission field itself.

Three goals of the French royal settlement shaped the growth of the Jesuit mission: to become familiar with the region and its resources, to encourage financial investment and migration from France to a worthy outpost of the mother country abroad, and to engage the Native peoples. Actual mission operations found themselves tugged in two sometimes rival, sometimes complementary, directions: to evangelize the Indigenous populations and to provide religious support for the French colonial population. The Jesuit preference was for activities related to the Native populations. The evangelizing work of Francis Xavier in Asia (1506–52) had captured all Europe's attention and inspired many fresh recruits to the order. A popular hope in France for comparable results in its colonies led to financial, popular, and political support for Jesuit works in New France. Jesuit leaders hoped not to have to choose between reaching out to the Indigenous peoples and providing for the spiritual and educational well-being of the settlers. They recognized that serving the French colonial population ensured the political sympathy and financial support needed to make progress in their evangelizing mission to Native Americans. But it was never clear what was the best balance to strike.

Jesuit activities—in Indigenous missions and in religious service to European settlers—thus progressed in parallel. Building on an alliance between the colonial government and Algonquin tribes, fur traders developed a system of moving into the interior with Native guides that put them in contact with Indigenous peoples, whose languages and cultures they began learning, and who introduced them to the geography and natural resources of the region. Jesuits joined them, and by this route moved deep into the continent's interior. How Native communities welcomed the missionaries correlated to how they viewed France as a potential economic and political ally. The explorations of Jacques Marquette (1637–75) in the 1660s and 1670s are the most famous of such travels. His work represents a high point of Jesuit involvement in the scientific and cartographic investigations of territories that were new to the Europeans. His explorations pushed the frontier of French familiarity with the continent westward. Aided by the Illinois people, he and the explorer Louis Jolliet were the first Europeans to map the northern origins of the Mississippi River. The new French foundations of Sault Ste. Marie and St. Ignace (now in Michigan) followed upon Marquette's travels.

The Jesuits were hopeful that their school in Quebec could attract Native children. Its curriculum consisted of both religious catechesis and the humanities. Instruction was multilingual. By the 1640s, however, the hope of recruiting Native children as boarders remained unfulfilled: Native Americans did not take well either to the curriculum, which provided skills that were largely irrelevant once they returned home, or to the classroom style, which was as foreign to local populations as it was familiar to the colonists. Native parents were reluctant to send their children to distant Quebec for an education of questionable value back home. The Jesuits also noticed that the schooling was not having the desired effects once the children returned home—that is, the Christianization of their families and communities. In consequence, the Jesuits gradually reoriented the school to serving predominantly the French settler families. The early Jesuits also recruited women religious to the colony to serve Native and settler populations. The Ursulines arrived in 1639, for example; and led by Sister Marie of the Incarnation, they opened the colony's first educational institution for women. Three Augustinian sisters arrived from Dieppe the same year and founded the colony's first hospital, L'Hôtel-Dieu de Québec.

Although the Jesuits had mixed success in their early educating enterprises, they were more characteristically successful at engaging in locally focused research and at disseminating that new knowledge back home. Among the most important pieces of research were *Customs of the American Indians compared with the Customs of Primitive Times* (1724) by Joseph-François Lafitau (1681–1746) and *The History and General Description*

FIGURE 1.3 "An Eclipse, biblical, ancient Roman, and Native views compared," from Joseph-François Lafitau's *Mœurs des sauvages américains comparées aux mœurs des premiers temps* (Paris, 1724). Lafitau set side by side an interpretive sketch of native ceremonies occasioned by eclipses and imagery taken from the biblical Book of Revelation. He used the juxtaposition to draw parallels and distinctions between astronomical events, like eclipses, and the symbols of dragons and virgins in native, ancient Roman, and Christian thought. Source: Illustration from *Mœurs des sauvages américains comparées aux mœurs des premiers temps*, by Joseph-François Lafitau (Paris, 1724), plate 13, volume 1, page 250. BFCSC, JG Shea Library, E58.L16 1724.

of New France (1744) by Pierre-François-Xavier de Charlevoix (1682–1761). Lafitau offered his readers a generalized description of Indigenous cultures along with an awkward but unambiguous defense of Indigenous customs as no more bizarre than many historical European ones. Charlevoix's work was an early, comprehensive geographical and geological narrative description of New France based on journeys funded by the French Crown.

The most famous set of reports from New France are the so-called *Jesuit Relations*. The *Relations* are a collection of reports and notices, composed as annual letters from the Jesuits in the colony to their superiors in France. They recount in minute detail their missionary activities. Jesuit superiors edited the reports from the missionaries for public consumption and distributed them serially across France between 1632 and 1673. They were immensely popular. They inspired many French to join the Society and others to volunteer to help the Society in the colonies. The letters encouraged further French settlement in New France. Scholars especially value these documents today as an unequalled documentary resource for the study of seventeenth-century Indigenous cultures. As the historian Allan Greer put it, "the Jesuits knew what they were talking about." They embedded themselves deeply in Native communities, learned their languages, and were keen observers. Even when the Jesuits did not approve of or understand what in the cultures they described as "diabolical" and "pagan," they still wrote about it in accurate detail, and at length. The letters' contents can still capture the imagination of a reader today, such as when Brebeuf advises a prospective missionary never to pick up a canoe paddle unless he is prepared to paddle all day; when Lalemant recounts one Native chief's promise at a peace conference that the French would now be able to eat "real meat" instead of that of "the pigs which run free in your towns, eating nothing but filth"; and when Marquette warns against close encounters with strange, bearded cattle (bison), which "when attacked, catch a man on their horns, if they can, toss him in the air, and then throw him on the ground, trample him under foot, and kill him."

As the Jesuits struggled in the late 1630s to recruit Native people to their Quebec school, they also were experimenting with founding villages for them in the model of the reductions in New Spain. The Jesuit reductions to the south, started in 1609, were settlements for Amerindians that had as goals the Christianization and Europeanization of the local populations as well as their protection from the Spanish and Portuguese slave trade. The first of the French reductions appeared along the Saint Lawrence River in and around Quebec City for the Algonquin and Wyandot (Huron). There were inducements to move into the reductions, such as discounts at French shops, and protective laws, such as a prohibition on the sale of liquor. This enterprise in New France was not long-lived. The situation in New France differed in decisive ways from that in New Spain, where 200,000 Native people lived in reductions by the mid–eighteenth century. In particular, the nomadic movements of the northern tribes disinclined them from settling in colonial villages, and the less exploitative attitude of French authorities than of Spanish and Portuguese ones toward Native communities lowered the attraction of the reductions as a haven. Moreover, British military harassment continued to impede Jesuit missionary work with Indigenous peoples throughout the mid–seventeenth century.

One of these reduction-like villages came to a particularly violent end, the village of Ste. Marie in the Wendake. The regional inhabitants, the Wyandot, were a largely agricultural and sedentary tribe, allied with the French. The Jesuit Brebeuf was living with the Wyandot when the mission superior Jerome Lalemant (1593–1673) decided that a reduction should be founded to encourage evangelization and to buffer the Wyandots from rival tribes and hostile European powers. Conversions—that goal so elusive in Quebec City and in the villages along the Saint Lawrence—slowly followed the establishment of Ste. Marie in 1639. In the ten months straddling 1643 and 1644, 120 baptisms were recorded. In 1648, nine years from its founding, the Ste. Marie population included twenty-three Jesuits, twenty-three lay French volunteers, and two hundred Christian Wyandot.

Rivalries between the French, the British, and the Dutch exacerbated rivalries among the Native communities, and hostilities broke out in the territory of the Wyandot in 1648. Over an eighteen-month period, Iroquois, armed by the Dutch, stormed the region. By 1650, six Jesuits had been captured and executed; one thousand Wyandot, enslaved; and Ste. Marie, torched and abandoned. War and disease reduced the Wyandot population in this period from 30,000 to several hundred. Fifteen years after the destruction of this mission, the colonial governor sent the Jesuit Simon Le Moyne (1604–65) on a peace mission to the Iroquois. In 1666 the Iroquois invited French Jesuits to join them. In the context of this new alliance, the nineteen-year-old Algonquin-Mohawk woman Tekakwitha (1656–80) received baptism. Given the Christian name Kateri (after Catherine of Siena), she moved to the Jesuit mission at Kahnawake, south of Montreal on the Saint Lawrence. There she followed an austere penitential regimen of life that drew from both Christian and Mohawk traditions of self-mortification.

Some activities continued into the eighteenth century in Acadia (then part of New France, now encompassed within Maine, the Canadian Maritime provinces, and Gaspesia). The territory was important to the French because of its frontier with English colonial Massachusetts. From the colonizing perspective, the local Indigenous people, the Abenakis, were a valuable chess piece in the French contest there with Britain, one that also was the object of the missionaries' evangelizing efforts. The French colonial government thus supported Catholic missions in the region and along that frontier in the interest of securing and expanding its claim over Acadia. The initial efforts of Pierre Biard (1567–1622), who arrived to establish contact with the Abenakis in 1611, were brought to an end by roving Virginians, who raided the region, kidnapped Biard with three confreres, and destroyed both the mission at Saint Sauveur and the colonial outpost at Port Royal. Biard ultimately returned to France. While his direct efforts in the mission failed, his *Relation of 1616*, a description of his experience and the missionizing potential of the region that he penned after returning to France, inspired considerable interest in returning to the region.

In this early period, it is sometimes difficult to distinguish service to the faith and to the empire. The life and death of Sébastien Rale (1657–1724) is a case in point. Rale spent over three decades in New France. He worked extensively in Abenaki communities near Quebec and in Acadia. He mastered their language, drafted a dictionary of it, and composed a catechism in it. In the conflicts over the border between English Massachusetts and French Acadia, the British increasingly suspected Rale of agitating the Native populations against them. In 1724, during a set of skirmishes and raids sometimes called "Father Rale's War," British forces attacked the Abenaki settlement where Rale resided. The surviving Abenaki were scattered; and Rale was killed and his scalp, sent to Boston. Nineteenth-century historians expressed a certain ambivalence about Rale on the matter of his intentions. It would be unsurprising that Francis Parkman, a Boston Unitarian whose history writing consistently celebrated in the rise of the United States the triumph of Anglo-Saxon Protestant energy and rationality over Catholic savagery and superstition, summarized Rale as "hating the English more than he loved the Indian; calling himself their friend, yet using them as instruments of worldly policy, to their danger and final ruin." But even John Gilmary Shea, Parkman's near exact contemporary and his foremost Catholic counterpart as a historian, acknowledged that

if [Rale's] national feeling as a Frenchman ever led him to overstep the bounds of prudence at the suggestion of the French king and the governor of Canada, with whom he was in constant correspondence, and who urged him, as we well know, to continue his opposition to English encroachment, there is, on the other hand, no doubt as to the injustice of New England to his flock, and of their bitter hatred to him personally on mere religious grounds, which prompted their unrelenting efforts to take his life.

The early eighteenth-century English military victories ended the Jesuit mission to the Abenaki, and the order did not reestablish itself in the territory until the next century, this time on a mission organized from the south.

The summary balance sheet on Jesuit activities in New France is a complicated one. Their work with Native populations remained fragile throughout the eighteenth century until British military victory, French royal decree, and papal suppression led to the mission's demise. The French Jesuits met mixed success in their goal of building a Christian Indigenous society and protecting it from colonial exploitation. Successes are found in individual cases, but the corporate project ended sadly. In contrast, their work among the settlers grew steadily. Although the Jesuits themselves were hobbled by anti-Catholic legislation once France lost the colony to the British in 1763, the parochial and educational institutions they ran continued operating afterward in the hands of others. We see in the work of the French Jesuits what we will see again and again in North American Jesuit activity: the Jesuits undertook enterprises with ambition and energy but also with limited personnel and resources. The Jesuit enterprises were never purely Jesuit operations—there were other secular and ecclesiastical influences and resources; and the ideals the men carried with them, usually drawn from South American and Asian missionary examples, were not entirely applicable to the situation in New France. Finally, the Jesuits in New France, like those in La Florida, offer an example of the change-in-course that shaped the Jesuit efforts in upper North America recurrently: The great attraction to the colonial missions—the evangelization of Native peoples, had to yield to another great enterprise, the spiritual care and education of the European settler.

English Maryland

After English colonial foundations at Jamestown in Virginia in 1607 and at Plymouth in Massachusetts in 1620, a third group of English colonists founded Saint Mary's City in Maryland in 1634. Among them were three Jesuits: two priests, Andrew White (1579–1656) and John Altham (1589–1640), and a lay brother, Thomas Gervase (1590–1637). What was so remarkable about this Jesuit involvement was its open existence in territory controlled by the English Crown. Jesuits arrived in New Spain and New France with the approval and support of the "most Catholic" and "most Christian" kings, as the crowned heads of Spain and France were respectively known. In contrast, being a Jesuit priest in territory under the jurisdiction of the English Crown was a crime, and in certain circumstances a capital offense. Many Jesuits, along with other Catholics, accordingly suffered execution under the Cross of Saint George. The actual terms and enforcement of penal laws against Catholics in England varied from moment to moment and from place to place, but the situation was never easy. An exiled Catholic population consequently emerged on the European continent with centers of activity in northern France, Spain, and Rome.

The creation of a colony with legal toleration for Catholics unfolded under the Stuart monarchs James I and Charles I in the early seventeenth century. Regardless of a relative sympathy on the part of the Stuarts to their Catholic subjects in comparison to that of their predecessor Queen Elizabeth I, English law required office holders at key intervals to take oaths acknowledging the king's absolute sovereignty, including over the Church, and denying the pope's authority to depose princes, endorse war, or absolve oaths. The intent of such a requirement was to exclude Catholics from high office and undermine the authority of the pope over Catholics. In 1625, George Calvert, a member of parliament and of the king's Privy Council, began to publicly profess his Catholicism. Calvert came from a Catholic family in Yorkshire but had publicly conformed to the Church of England to enter a university and then to rise in royal service. His reversion to Catholicism obliged him to remove himself from Parliament and put his position at the royal court in jeopardy. James I, as a marker of confidence, created for him the Barony of Baltimore (a castle in Ireland) and promised him a charter for a colony in

North America. At the succession of Charles to his father James later in 1625, members of the Privy Council were required to renew their oaths. When the council assembled to do so, Calvert and another Catholic councilor were absent and were accordingly discharged from office.

George Calvert spent the remaining seven years of his life attempting and failing to establish settlements in Newfoundland and Virginia. In the midst of new plans for a settlement north of the Virginia colony, he died in 1632. His title and colonial patent fell to his eldest son, Cecil. George's second son, Leonard, led the family's next, ultimately successful expedition to North America and governed on site in his brother's name. The brothers continued their father's goal of founding a colony that would accommodate Catholic settlers, among whom could be priests in their service. George had already invited Jesuits to participate in his expedition to Newfoundland. The Jesuit Andrew White, a sometime underground priest in Britain and sometime theology instructor on the continent, befriended George in the late 1620s. White helped negotiate the Jesuit participation in the sons' colonial plans. The superior general in Rome gave his blessing to the new English mission in December 1633, several weeks after Calvert's ships had set sail for Maryland with White and the others aboard.

Naming their colony after King Charles I's Catholic wife Henrietta Maria, the Calverts were determined to signal their loyalty to the English Crown and not to antagonize Protestants, despite the presence of Catholics among the colonists. Jesuits thus traveled to the colony not as clergy per se but, like the other elite colonists, as "gentlemen adventurers." According to the "Conditions of Plantation," the contract between the Calverts and the colonists, gentlemen adventurers received land in the colony in proportion to the number of laborers they brought with them. Thus, instead of receiving support directly from the colonial government, as an established church might (and in contrast, for example, to the French Western Company's arrangement to support Jesuits in the Louisiana mission in the 1720s with salaries and church buildings), the Jesuits were promised land. With the

laborers they also recruited to the colony, they could then support themselves and their ministries with the revenues generated
by farming. The first two ships, the *Ark* and the *Dove*, carried
about 150 persons, of whom only a minority were Catholic. They
arrived in the Chesapeake Bay in early 1634. The colonists began making contacts with the local Yaocomico and Piscataway,
Algonquian peoples distantly related to those with whom the
French Jesuits were in contact in New France. Their arrival was
formally marked with a Mass on March 25, the Feast of the
Annunciation and the beginning of the general calendar year by
English reckoning at the time, on an island in the Potomac River
that they named after the patron of mariners, Saint Clement.
They established their colonial capital, Saint Mary's City, on a
nearby tributary of the Potomac.

Like so many of their confreres drawn to New Spain and New
France, the English Jesuits were eager to contact the Native peoples.
White himself first settled at some remove from Saint Mary's to be
in closer contact with them. Into the late 1630s, White translated
prayers into the Piscataway language and worked on a dictionary
and grammar. The Piscataway emperor (*tayac*), Kittamaquund,
accepted baptism in 1640; others in the tribe followed suit. A
formal mission to the Piscataway, however, never came to be.
The colonial governor was adamant that the Jesuits serve first
the Catholic settlers. He also expressed concern over the safety
of Jesuits in the field, who might find themselves in danger from
either Indigenous peoples or from what was in fact more often the
case, the English settlers of neighboring colonies, disturbed at the
idea of Catholics living, worshipping, and proselytizing on their
borders. Conflicts among Native communities further hampered
the Jesuits' relationship with the Piscataway. Over the course of
the seventeenth century, the Piscataway moved westward under
pressure from another group, the Susquehannocks, who took
their place in the territory of southern Maryland and were themselves uninclined to contact with the English.

The Jesuits therefore spent most of their mission activities
tending to the religious and educational needs of the settlers. This

included celebration of the sacraments and administration of the Spiritual Exercises, the program of meditations and prayers developed by the order's founder, Saint Ignatius. But the two most striking features of the Jesuit mission to Maryland are, as has been suggested, not to be found in the kind of works the Jesuits undertook, which were similar to their projects in other colonies and across Europe, but rather in the legal conditions under which they worked and the means that supported them. Given the hostility in English law toward Catholics, and their clergy in particular, the compromise worked out by the Calverts is striking, not just for England but Europe generally: The Calverts had in effect proposed a model of state-sanctioned religious pluralism with toleration for all Christians. In the Thirteen Colonies, the Calvert model distinguished itself from the more limited religious toleration to be found in Pennsylvania and Rhode Island, to say nothing of Puritan Massachusetts and Anglican Virginia, where established churches excluded Catholics and penalized nonconforming Protestants. Indeed, the Calverts' religious toleration surpassed in practice the toleration John Locke proposed in theory a half century later, which specifically excluded Catholics. In Maryland the legislature went so far as to extend religious liberty to all regardless of confession. Such expansive religious toleration did not last long. Cromwell's Puritan revolution in Britain ten years later made it expedient for the Maryland colony to make its toleration less provocative. Nonetheless, by reducing toleration still to include those who confessed belief in the Trinity, the Maryland Act of Toleration (1649) was the widest standard in the British colonies and did encompass Catholics.

As Cromwell's influence on Maryland's religious toleration offers evidence, religious and political tensions at home reverberated in the colonies. In this period of tumultuous conflict between kings, who were Anglican, and Parliament, which sympathized with more radical forms of Protestantism, Catholics tended to see their fate in Maryland tied to the king's; and many Protestants, with Parliament's. This mid-seventeenth-century religious and political conflict resulted in one especially violent interruption in the

Jesuit presence in Maryland: Puritans whom the Catholic governor had earlier allowed to settle on the Severn River as refugees from persecutions in Virginia joined forces with a Virginia governor in 1645 to raid the Maryland capital, plunder Catholic property, and transport what Jesuits they could arrest back to Britain for prosecution. The privateer Richard Ingle captured five Jesuits, including White and Thomas Copley (1596–1652). Of the five, three were put ashore in hostile Susquehannock territory and were never seen again. White and Copley were returned to England in chains. There, the defendants argued that as they had been brought back by force they were not willingly violating England's prohibition of priests on the island. Copley additionally argued that the capital crime did not apply to him, since he was not native born, but born in Spain. The court accepted their arguments and banished them, admonishing them never to return under pain of death. After a brief stay on the European continent, White returned not to Maryland but to England, where he lived out his days serving the Catholic population underground. Once the Calverts' control of the colony was reestablished in 1648, Copley returned to Maryland.

Over the course of the next century and a quarter, the legal and social status of Catholics wavered back and forth, and thus of the Jesuits, too. Once William of Orange and Mary Stuart succeeded to the throne following the ouster of James II in 1688, penal laws were again enforced in Maryland in earnest. Protestants in the colony were emboldened to move the capital from Saint Mary's to Annapolis, the town on the Severn earlier founded as a refuge for Puritans from Virginia. Catholic churches were locked up and services were prohibited. Catholics were taxed to support the Anglican clergy, were deprived of the vote and excluded from holding public office, were forbidden to inherit property unless they swore the oath of allegiance, were fined for sending their children abroad to be educated in Catholic schools, and were taxed to compensate for their prohibited service in the militia. Expulsion of the Catholic population, however, was neither feasible nor, to the colonial leadership, desirable. The effects of religious intolerance at any given moment were always tempered by the practical *convivencia* that had sustained the Maryland project since the beginning. Intermarriage of the sons and daughters of leading Catholic and Protestant families likewise contributed to mutual appreciation, as had the full cooperation of the Jesuits at work in the colony in the practice of legal religious toleration. Jesuits thus managed to operate discreetly even during the reign of William and Mary. A breakthrough was reached under Queen Anne (r. 1702–14): the Maryland authorities determined that the Catholics, while prohibited from having churches, could worship in house chapels, defined as having their principal entrance within a larger building rather than on the street.

The second distinctive feature of the Maryland mission, related to the first, was its system of financial support. While the mission benefited from the charity of Catholic families, the land they received according to Calvert's "Conditions of Plantations" was to be its ordinary source of funding. This solved one political problem but opened up an ecclesiastical one: according to the Jesuits' own law, only houses of training for Jesuits and colleges could operate with revenue-generating land, not missions such as Maryland. To solve this problem, a paper transfer was arranged: the Maryland land revenues were assigned to a Jesuit college operating in hiding in London. That college then returned the revenues as "alms," a charitable contribution, to the Maryland mission.

The land grants also shaped the organization of the mission itself. Distributed in parcels, the multiple large plots concentrated Jesuits at three geographical points in the colony, all along the Potomac River. Those estates became the hubs of religious activity, and management of the estates became the principal activity of a core group of priests and brothers. These exigencies—the rural situation of the Jesuits and the hostility toward Catholics across the colonies—in turn shaped the outreach to Catholics beyond Maryland. In the neighboring colony of Pennsylvania, a first urban church in the mission—Saint Joseph in Philadelphia—was founded in 1732, nearly a century after White disembarked on the Potomac. Joseph Greaton (1679–1753) purchased the land surreptitiously. When the purpose was discovered, the Quaker governor convened his council in emergency session to determine whether such a purchase and use of land by Catholics were legal. The city fathers determined that they were. But for the sake of public order, the building could incorporate no public indications of its Catholic usage: the church was to have no bell tower, no entrance onto a main street, and no "graven images"—stained glass of saints, for example—visible from the main street. From Philadelphia, the Jesuits were able to develop outreach into rural Pennsylvania and New York, where recent waves of German immigration included Catholics.

Anti-Catholicism and a rural focus shaped the Jesuit educational enterprise as well. Two attempts were made to operate schools at the mission church Saint Xavier at Newtown on the Potomac. Neither lasted long. Both suffered from a lack of students and instructors. The second school was forced to close in 1698 on account of new legislation prohibiting Catholics from operating schools. Taking advantage of what proved to be the brief tenure of a Catholic governor in New York, the English Jesuits attempted to operate a mission in New York between 1683 and 1689. At the height of their efforts, the missionaries made a proposal—one that was returned to again and again over the next centuries and, this time, rejected—that the headquarters of all Jesuit activity on the continental east coast be moved from Maryland to New York. With other Jesuits, Thomas Harvey (1635–96) even recruited students with the aim of starting a college in the colonial capital city, but without success. Then, the turmoil in Britain that resolved with William and Mary's crowning led to the governor's removal and ended Jesuit activity in New York City in the colonial period.

Finally, the Jesuits founded their longest-lasting educational institution in the colonial period at the mission station in Bohemia, Maryland, on the northeastern shore of the Chesapeake Bay in 1745. The Bohemia Academy stayed open into the early years of the Republic. It provided only a primary education. Beyond that, opportunities for Catholics were few. While Protestant families could take advantage of a growing educational infrastructure across the English colonies, especially to the north, penal laws and popular prejudice hindered the matriculation of Catholics. This restricted further education for Catholics to the families who could afford sending their sons to Europe, where the school at Saint-Omer in French Flanders served the English Catholics in exile. This, for example, was the route taken by John Carroll (1735–1815), the scion of a prominent Catholic family in Maryland who became a Jesuit and later the first Catholic bishop in the United States. The first institution of advanced learning not under sectarian direction was Benjamin Franklin's "University of the State of Pennsylvania" (now the University of Pennsylvania), among whose earliest trustees numbered Ferdinand Farmer (1720–86), the superior of the Saint Joseph mission in the 1770s and 1780s.

In addition to the difficulty in managing the lands supporting the Jesuit mission, another challenge had to do simply with ownership. The colonial charter and legislation recognized no mortmain, meaning there was no provision for institutions, like churches, as incorporations to own property. Land in the colony ordinarily changed hands by sale, gift, and inheritance. Individual Jesuits had no legal heirs, and the custom in Catholic countries of priests' designating their religious order as their heir had no legal legitimacy in Maryland. Furthermore, penal laws made ownership and inheritance of property by Catholics difficult and punitively expensive. Land held by priests was at particular risk of confiscation. Thus, there was no easy, reliable way for the Jesuit property to be held together as a unit. A working solution emerged in the form of trusteeship: colonial families, sometimes even amenable Protestant ones, held the properties in trust for the Jesuits. Trusteeship allowed the Jesuit holdings to be kept intact throughout the colonial period.

By the end of the seventeenth century, the mission property included not only land, buildings, livestock, and farming equipment but also enslaved people. At first, the colony's labor force came under terms of indentured servitude. Such laborers agreed to work for a certain number of years in exchange for transportation to the colonies, and at the end of their tenure, for a parcel of land. They were provided with food, clothing, and shelter as they worked off the terms of the contract in the colony, usually as farmhands. Most indentured servants in Maryland were of European origin. The first Maryland resident of African descent, Mathias de Sousa, was one of the thirty indentured servants brought to the colony by the Jesuits in 1634 under the "Conditions of Plantation." De Sousa completed his contract by 1641, and afterward worked on a trading vessel and even served in the colonial legislature. As the seventeenth century progressed, the growing demand for farm labor across British North America, including Maryland, outstripped the supply of indentured servants in Europe. The first enslaved Africans arrived in Maryland in 1642. The same Maryland legislature that drafted liberal laws of religious toleration also drafted new laws excluding from the enslaved Africans the legal rights of free men and indentured servants. Over the course of the seventeenth century, indentured servitude gave way to chattel slavery across the colony. This transition occurred on the Jesuit plantations without explanatory note in the Jesuits' otherwise copious archival records.

The number of enslaved people owned at any one time by the Jesuits in upper North America approached 300 in the mid–eighteenth century. French Jesuits owned up to one hundred enslaved persons in the Mississippi River Valley, some of them also from Native communities. But the majority labored on the farms of the Maryland mission. The English Jesuits acquired slaves by bequest, gift, exchange, and purchase. Enslaved families increased in size over time, thus augmenting the number of the enslaved the Jesuits owned. Chattel slavery in the British colonies was a brutal system, and Jesuits enforced their control over the enslaved with typical violence, which included beatings, floggings, and the sale of runaways. Slaves judged unnecessary were likewise sold off, sometimes without regard to age or family connections. The revenue generated by this slave trading was used to support Jesuit communities and works across the colonies. Jesuits, contrary to ordinary slave-holding practice in the English colonies, encouraged the enslaved people to accept baptism and provided catechesis. The Jesuits kept sacramental records of baptisms, marriages, and burials, many of which are still extant. Some of the enslaved people learned rudimentary reading and writing. When the pope suppressed the Jesuit order in 1773, mission property was held together for the use of the remaining Church through trusteeship and, ultimately, a process of legal incorporation in the new, independent State of Maryland. When a new Jesuit mission was established in Maryland in the early nineteenth century, it gradually acquired control over the incorporated property, including enslaved people.

Between 1611 and 1773, fewer than two hundred Jesuits served in upper North America. The prospect of evangelizing Native peoples was the principal attraction drawing Jesuits to both French and British colonies. Service to the settlers, in contrast, was what made the Jesuits attractive to the colonial authorities. Founding educational institutions was also common in both regions from the very beginning. A tension between working with Native peoples and serving the settlers surfaced again and again. By the middle of the eighteenth century, both English and French Jesuits could look at their present moment with qualified satisfaction, but also with fear: For the French Jesuits, the transfer of the colony from France to Britain resulted in the same legal prejudices that the English Jesuits had faced since their arrival. Even more consequentially, the French Jesuits were facing hostility at home in the 1760s that ultimately led to their suppression by royal decree in France and its colonies. For the English Jesuits, the papal suppression of the order coincided with the outbreak of revolt against the Crown in thirteen British colonies. That papal suppression left the twenty-one Jesuits in the Thirteen Colonies without any organizing structure; and America's War of Independence made it unclear whence new direction for the small Church would come. What happens to these ecclesiastical orphans is the topic of our next chapter.

FURTHER READING

Primary Literature

Jesuit Relations [*Relations de ce qui s'est passé de plus remarquable aux missions des Pères de la Compagnie de Jésus en la Nouvelle-France*]. These annual letters from the Jesuits in New France to their superiors in France recount in minute detail colonial life and missionary activity in New France. They include the reactions of the white colonists and accounts of aboriginal life and culture. The letters were edited for public consumption and distributed serially across France, where they were avidly read. They inspired many French to join the Society, and others to volunteer to help the Society in the colonies. The letters encouraged further French settlement in New France. Ethnographers and historians regard the *Relations* as a trove for study of the colonial experience and a resource for the recovery of precontact Native American culture:

- *Monumenta Novae Franciae*. Edited by Lucien Campeau. Rome: Institutum Historicum Societatis Jesu, 1967ff. Each document is published in its original language (French, Italian, Latin), with annotations in French. Many documents unknown to Thwaites (infra) are incorporated into the *Monumenta*.

- *Jesuit Relations and Allied Documents*. Edited by Reuben Gold Thwaites. Cleveland: Burrow Brothers, 1896–1901. Letters are published in their original language, with an English translation on facing pages. The annotations are in English.

- *The Jesuit Relations: Natives and Missionaries in Seventeenth-Century North America*, 2nd edition. Boston: Bedford / St. Martin's Press, 2019. The Canadian historian Allan Greer has prepared this very fine edition of selected materials from the *Relations*. Arranged by theme, his introductions to the documents are especially helpful.

- Hughes, Thomas. *History of the Society of Jesus in North America, Colonial and Federal: Documents*. Two parts. Cleveland: Burrows Brothers, 1908, 1910. These volumes include hundreds of transcribed documents, dating from 1605 to 1838, with succinct introductions. Hughes also produced two accompanying volumes of narrative history, which begin with the Jesuit fathers Edmund Campion and Robert Parson's "safe penetration into the kingdom [of England] on June 12, 1580" and concludes with the Suppression.

- There are several printings of Andrew White's sea voyage to and arrival in the Maryland Colony; for example, Hughes (supra) includes the document in his collection. The Archives of Maryland and the Library of Congress both maintain online versions of "A Briefe Relation of the Voyage unto Maryland."

Secondary Literature

Balláriaux, Catherine. *Missionary Strategies in the New World, 1610–1690: An Intellectual History*. New York: Routledge, Taylor & Francis, 2016. This hard-to-find study offers an exquisite analysis of missionary efforts in North, Central, and South America that—by encompassing Catholic and Reformed, French, Spanish, and British activities—is innovatingly comparative and comprehensive. Similarly insightful are Balláriaux's reconstructions of interpretations and practice of everyday mission life with reference to the theological foundations of the distinct Catholic and Reformed impulse to convert.

Boyton, James. *Fishers of Men: The Jesuit Mission at Mackinac, 1670–1765*. Mackinac Island, MI: Ste. Anne's Church, 1996. This focused, archivally based study of the mission of Saint Ignace de Missilimackinac offers microhistorical insight into the French missionary enterprise on the Great Lakes. Boyton (1967–), himself a Jesuit and part Native American, analyzes multiple facets of the history with subtlety in this slender volume.

Breidenbach, Michael D. *Our Dear-Bought Liberty: Catholics and Religious Toleration in Early America*. Cambridge, MA: Harvard University Press, 2021. Breidenbach investigates how Catholics in the colonial and early federal periods negotiated legal and social religious intolerance and contributed to emerging notions of religious tolerance in law and society.

Curran, R. Emmett. *Papist Devils: Catholics in British North America, 1574–1783*. Washington, DC: Catholic University of America Press, 2014. Curran puts the Catholics of the Maryland colony in a larger framework that encompasses the British Caribbean and Canada. Curran (1936–, left 1998) was a Jesuit of the Maryland province.

Greer, Allan. *Mohawk Saint: Catherine Tekakwitha and the Jesuits*. Oxford: Oxford University Press, 2005. *Mohawk Saint* is a dual biography of Katéri Tekakwitha and the Jesuit missionary Claude Chauchetière. The microhistory illuminates the complementary complexities of Jesuit missionary intentions and their effects on Indigenous peoples, whose own voices are so difficult to reconstruct.

Lewis, Clifford Merle, and Albert J. Loomie. *The Spanish Jesuit Mission in Virginia, 1570–1572*. Chapel Hill: University of North Carolina Press, 1953. While related historical issues and relevant methods have developed since the publication of *Spanish Jesuit Mission*, it offers to date the only sustained scholarly treatment of this episode in the Jesuit history of North America.

McShea, Bronwen. *Apostles of Empire: The Jesuits and New France*. Lincoln: University of Nebraska Press, 2019. In this revisionist history of Jesuit missions in New France, McShea is attentive to the intertwining of the political and the religious in all that the French Jesuits attempted in their seventeenth- and eighteenth-century New World ventures.

2

Suppression, 1762–1840

I N JESUIT HISTORY, the Suppression refers to the forty-one
years from 1773 to 1814, during which period the Society of
Jesus lost its ecclesiastical standing as a religious order. The
Suppression began and ended with papal decrees: Clement XIV's
"breve" *Dominus ac Redemptor* (*Lord and Redeemer*, 1773),
which abolished the Society, and Pius VII's "bull" *Sollicitudo omnium ecclesiarum* (*The Care of All the Churches*, 1814), which
reestablished it in Church law. (A bull is a more authoritative
papal decree than a breve: the pope himself signs a bull; an assistant, usually a cardinal, signs a breve on the pope's behalf.)
According to the breve of suppression, Jesuit priests were to report to their nearest bishops to serve as parish priests or apply
to another religious congregation, the unordained were released
from their vows, and Jesuit property devolved to the local bishop.
What actually happened, however, was far more complex than
what the breve gives to understand.

The ecclesiastical abolition, in fact, followed the banishment
of Jesuits from several European states and their colonial empires: from Portugal in 1759, France in 1764, Spain in 1767, and
several Italian principalities in 1768. The "Jesuit question" over
what to do with the order in light of the hostility of absolutist
regimes and various ecclesiastical blocs dominated discussions
at the three-month-long papal conclave of 1769. That conclave

elected Clement XIV (r. 1769–74) whose candidacy the Society's opponents supported. Four years later, Clement issued *Dominus ac Redemptor*, explaining "we have further observed that the Society of Jesus no longer brings forth those most plentiful and abundant fruits and services for which it was established. . . . [Therefore] with complete understanding, certain knowledge, and a fullness of apostolic power we do abolish and suppress the said Society." Local bishops were responsible for putting *Dominus* into effect, but the approval and cooperation of the secular authorities was also necessary. The crowned heads of Catholic Europe aided in the implementation of *Dominus* with an enthusiasm unmatched in the history of papal edicts. The brutality of the Suppression—the imprisonment and banishment of individuals; the confiscation and spoliation of property and the capricious reassignment of ownership; and the incalculable damage to Western culture, learning, and care for the dispossessed in the closing of Jesuit works—is well documented.

And yet, two major European powers, within whose jurisdiction Jesuits were legally working in 1773, did not cooperate with Clement's decree. In Prussia and Russia, neither sovereign—Frederick the Great and Catherine the Great—was Catholic, nor inclined to acquiesce to a papal demand. Both also wanted to keep the Jesuit schools open in territory they had newly acquired by their recent seizures of Polish territory. While the pope ultimately persuaded Frederick to enforce a dissolution of the religious order that allowed the ex-Jesuit priests to continue running schools, the Tsarina was not so compromising. The domestic benefit of keeping the order active was clearer to her. "It is our supreme will that the Jesuits live in our Empire, conserve their ancient manner of life, and continue to teach in their colleges," she decreed. She even rejected the local Jesuit superior's request to be suppressed: "I see that you are overscrupulous," she responded, "I will communicate with my Ambassador at Warsaw and have him reach an understanding with the papal nuncio to free you from your scruples." As a result, an enclave of Jesuits emerged in the Russian Empire, centered in the city of Polotsk (now in Belarus). They

FIGURE 2.1 Facade of the Jesuit college and church in Polotsk (the buildings have since been destroyed; the city was then in the Russian Empire and is now in Belarus). The Jesuits established a college in Polotsk in 1580, which operated until 1820, when Emperor Alexander II banished the Jesuits from the Russian Empire. During the Suppression, Polotsk became the principal house of the Society, housing a novitiate, a house of studies, and the remnant's curia. Giovanni Grassi and Anthony Kohlman, among others who later served in the US mission, trained here. The second elected superior of the restored Society, Jan Roothaan, also entered the Society here; and after Pope Pius VII's *Catholicae fidei* (1801), a congregation (the fourth of the Russian period) held here elected the Austrian Gabriel Gruber the "superior general of the Society of Jesus in Russia." Gruber, as superior general, authorized the reestablishment of the Jesuits in the United States by letter to John Carroll in 1804. Source: Facade of the Jesuit college and church in Polotsk, Vilnius, Lithuania, Vilnius University Library, Manuscript Department, fonds F78-1011.

worked there without interruption during the Suppression; and in the meantime, Clement's successors, Pius VI (r. 1775–99) and Pius VII (r. 1800–1823), maneuvered to reestablish the order.

In Protestant Britain, the order was already banned. Despite its activity through loopholes in places such as Maryland, King George III took no inspiration from the papal brief to further persecute the Jesuits and even expressed sympathy at their expulsion from France. Given the circumstances of Catholics in Maryland, local authorities had little interest in a regional suppression. The vicar apostolic of the London district, who took responsibility for suppressing the Society in the colonies, left them there to work as parish priests. Changes in the status of the Russian Jesuits ultimately allowed the order to be restored in the United States a decade before *Sollicitudo*. For that short while, America became mission territory of the order in Russia. After *Sollicitudo*, America became a refuge for Jesuits of the reestablished order who found themselves unwelcomed by civil authorities in Europe. The aim of this chapter is to tell the unusual story of the Suppression and the Restoration in upper North America.

THE SUPPRESSION IN FRENCH TERRITORIES

By the mid–eighteenth century, Jesuit activity in the French colonies of continental North America was concentrated in two regions: Quebec and the southern Mississippi River Valley. During this period, the North American French territories were under sustained siege from the British in a conflict known as the French and Indian Wars. The contending powers concluded hostilities with the Treaty of Paris in February 1763. According to the treaty, the French lost all territory in upper North America, the British gained control of Quebec, and the Mississippi River became a new border separating British holdings to the east from Spanish holdings to the west. Concurrently, the Parlement of Paris (an appellate court, not a legislature) and the French Crown were engaged in a process of suppressing the Jesuit order across France, a process that culminated in Louis XV's decree in November 1764 that dissolved the Society throughout France and its colonies.

In July 1763 the French director general of Louisiana, whose responsibility it was to prepare New Orleans and the southern Mississippi River Valley for transfer to British and Spanish authorities, began implementation of the recent anti-Jesuit decrees. Enforcement was implemented in stages from New Orleans northward up the Mississippi River to Kaskaskia (today near and to the south of Saint Louis) and beyond. Colonial authorities seized all

Jesuit property. Sacred vessels were handed over to the Capuchin Franciscans. Real property and chattel, including enslaved people, were confiscated and sold at auction. When these revenues landed in French coffers, the British protested that by the terms of the treaty, such profits belonged to them, not the French. The Jesuit priests were ordered to serve the local bishop as parish clergy. The unordained, both scholastics and brothers, were left to fend for themselves. Some Jesuits took refuge in neighboring Spanish territory, where the order had not yet been suppressed. When it was suppressed there, too, the Franciscans took responsibility for Jesuit missions. A French ex-Jesuit, Louis Sebastian Meurin (1707–77), with the permission first of the Louisiana

Figure 2.2   San José de Tumacácori, Arizona. The Jesuit Eusebio Kino founded a mission in 1691 for the O'odham peoples. The inhabitants built and worshipped in an adobe structure, San Cayetano, which was abandoned when, after the Pima uprising of 1751, the mission was relocated to the other side of the Santa Cruz River. The new church was dedicated to San José. After the Spanish authorities expelled the Jesuits in 1767, the Franciscans took over many of the missions in the region. The friars withdrew from San José in 1848 and concentrated their efforts at another of Kino's foundations, San Xavier del Bac. Source: San José de Tumacácori, Arizona, Alamy Stock Photo / Susan E. Degginger, MW24WB.

Superior Council and then of the British, continued working in the Mississippi Valley until his death in 1777.

In contrast, Quebec came under British control more quickly after the Treaty of Paris. Accommodation was made for the Catholic population of Quebec, where churches stayed open and a bishop remained to govern the diocese. The British allowed religious orders such as the Society to continue their charitable works but prohibited them from admitting new novices. This regulation ensured their extinction. The last of the Jesuits in Quebec, Jean-Joseph Casot (1728–1800), died in 1800, and Jesuit properties devolved to the British government. The Jesuits did not return to Canada until 1842.

THE SUPPRESSION IN THE UNITED STATES

Three aspects of Catholic life in the lower colonies begin to account for the distinctive ways the suppression plays out there: First, Catholic colonists had well established detours to avoid the penal laws. Jesuits could usually administer the sacraments and even sometimes run a small school with little, or at least irregular, molestation from civil authorities. Second, while the Jesuits were benefiting from the usufruct of their land grants, ownership of the farms was often in the hands of lay trustees. Thus, one material incentive to enforcement of the papal bull—the expropriation of Jesuit property—was, in Maryland, diminished. And third, ecclesiastical jurisdiction over Maryland Catholics was somewhat confused. Other than the Jesuit order, two Church entities could claim jurisdiction over Catholics in the Thirteen Colonies: the Apostolic Vicariate of London, under which Catholics in British colonies fell; and the pope's Sacred Congregation for the Propagation of the Faith, which handled mission territories. Since the Jesuits up to 1773 had their own religious superiors, they had operated independently of both. With the order's governing structure gone, there was no suitable, convenient, or close bishop to whom the ordained former Jesuits could report. Recent military hostilities and the standing political tensions between the British and the French made the bishop of Quebec an unlikely mediator for any suppression of the Jesuits in Maryland. No more likely was the bishop of Santiago de Cuba, the nearest bishop to the south. Adding to all this uncertainty, tensions between the British Crown and the North American colonists were growing on account of tax increases. Riots and other protests against the Crown were breaking out just as the fate of the Society was being debated across Europe: the Boston Tea Party took place in 1773, the War of Independence broke out in 1775, and the (other) Treaty of Paris in 1783 acknowledged the independence of the Thirteen Colonies from Britain. In consequence, an apostolic prefecture, independent of the London vicariate, was created for the new nation in 1784.

But we are running ahead of ourselves. With the promulgation of *Dominus*, it fell to the vicar apostolic, Richard Challoner, to suppress the Maryland mission. He did just that, and the mission superior received the following letter in the fall of 1773: "To obey the orders I have rec[eive]d from above, I notify to you by this the Breve of the total dissolution of the Society of Jesus; and send withal a form of declaration of your obedience and submissions to which you are all desired to subscribe, as your brethren have done here, and send me back the formula with the subscriptions of you all, as I am to send them up to Rome."

There were, at this time, twenty-one Jesuit priests in the mid-Atlantic colonies, of whom three were Maryland natives. In addition, about two dozen American-born Jesuits were studying and working in Europe. As a result of *Dominus*, the priests became parish clergy, subject to the vicar apostolic. On the matter of the estates, in addition to the hindrances to land seizure mentioned above, the ex-Jesuits argued that cooperation with any effort to confiscate Jesuit property would constitute *praemunire*, that is, the crime in Protestant England of collaboration with foreign, papal authority, and an act of treason. The property thus remained as it had been, in the hands of trustees, ex-Jesuit and lay. It should be noted that at the time, there were no other Catholic clergy in the Thirteen Colonies besides the ex-Jesuits. Father John Lewis,

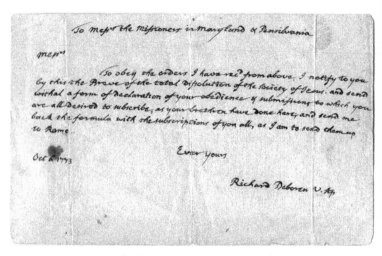

FIGURE 2.3   Notification of the Suppression to the Jesuits of the Maryland Mission from Richard Challoner, October 6, 1773: "To obey the orders I have received from above, I notify to you by this Breve of the total dissolution of the Society of Jesus, and send withal a form of declaration of your obedience and submissions to which you are all desired to subscribe, as your brethren have done here and send me back the formula with the subscriptions of you all, as I am to send them up to Rome. Ever yours, Richard, [bishop of] Debra, vicar apostolic [of London]." Challoner is better known today for his revision of the traditional Catholic English-vernacular Bible, the Douay-Rheims. Source: Notification of the Suppression to the Maryland Jesuits from Richard Challoner, BFCSC, Maryland Province Archives, 119 2 8.

who had been the last of the Jesuit mission superiors, continued in office, now as Bishop Challoner's vicar general. Based at eleven residences across Maryland and Pennsylvania, the ex-Jesuits were left to continue in their service to the 30,000 Catholic colonists (of a general population of 3 million).

The choice faced by the American-born Jesuits in Europe was whether to stay or to return to the colonies. Most returned. Among them was John Carroll (1735–1815). Both the Carrolls and the Darnells, his mother's family, were leading families in Maryland. Several family members played significant roles in the colonial movement for independence. Carroll's education models the best possible for Catholics in his day: his mother tutored him in his earliest years, preparing him to enter the Jesuit school on the upper Chesapeake Bay at Bohemia Manor. Upon completing that program at age thirteen, "Little Jackie" was sent to the college for English Catholics in exile at Saint-Omer in French Flanders. He entered the English province of the Jesuit order in 1753. He undertook his studies at Liège, and he was ordained in 1761. He taught thereafter at several schools in the Low Countries.

Carroll was at the college in Bruges with fellow American Charles Thompson when Austrian troops stormed the residence to arrest the Jesuits and seize the property. As Americans, the two were permitted to leave. While Thompson remained in Europe, Carroll made plans to return to Maryland. What he found upon his return in the summer of 1774 distressed him. No effective governing structure had arisen to fill the void left by the suppression of the Jesuit order. Rudderless, the old missionaries had become inattentive to even basic ministrations to the faithful; and lay Catholics, who had suffered under so many decades of penal laws and come to rely passively on the energies of the missionary order, were becoming all the more distant from their religion.

Although one must always be wary of identifying a single personality as the architect of major change, in this instance Carroll deserves considerable credit for the gradual but sure emergence of a vigorous Catholic Church in the period of early national independence. Upon his return, he began by working as a traveling missionary in Maryland and Virginia. His journeys connected him to a Catholic community from which he had been separated since his departure for France a quarter century earlier, and they familiarized him with the state of Catholicism in the colonies. Thanks to his prominent family, he developed friendships with leading figures in the movement for colonial independence. He accompanied the American founding fathers Benjamin Franklin and Samuel Chase in 1776 on a mission to recruit the Quebecois to the fight for independence from Britain. The diplomatic mission failed in its expressed aim, but it cemented domestic relationships that served the fledgling Church for decades to come.

His first major accomplishment in organizing the Church in the thirteen now independent states came in the summer of 1783; Carroll assembled the remaining priests in a so-called General Chapter at the White Marsh plantation in Maryland, a property that the Carrolls had bequeathed to the Jesuits earlier in the century. The participants drafted a constitution that divided the mission into three districts, directed the districts to select two representatives each, and established that these representatives—assembling as the Select Body of Clergy—should meet at regular intervals to assign personnel, administer property, and maintain ecclesiastical discipline. Two important early decisions of the Select Body were in 1784 to request that Rome name Carroll superior of the mission and in 1788 to found an academy for Catholics, the future Georgetown College (now Georgetown Preparatory School and Georgetown University), to alleviate the need to send young Catholic men to Europe for advanced schooling.

The Select Body also deliberated whether to request a bishop from Rome. Two factors militated against such a request: first, both an invigorated Evangelical piety and burgeoning republicanism inspired animosity toward the pretentions of high ecclesiastical office across the new country. The first American Methodist bishop, consecrated in 1784, refrained from using the title in his early years in office; and the first Episcopal bishop, who was consecrated in Scotland in 1785 to avoid an oath recognizing the king's supremacy over the Church, faced constant public harassment back home. Second, there was a latent mistrust among the ex-Jesuits toward the papal department that oversaw the appointment of bishops in mission territory, the Sacred Congregation for the Propagation of the Faith. Many ex-Jesuits, Carroll included, laid some blame for the Suppression on it. In the end, the Select Body decided to request a bishop from Rome in March 1788 for the sake of proper governance and the sacrament of Holy Orders, which only a bishop could administer. Rome's response was quick, affirmative, and authorized unusual next steps: the Select Body itself was to designate a first see and to name a candidate from among its own number to be presented to Rome for confirmation. Rome granted this irregular decision-making role to the Select Body to minimize the impression that the new bishop was the appointee of a foreign power. The Select Body elected Carroll first bishop of the newly designated See of Baltimore. Carroll traveled to Lulworth Castle in southwest England, where Bishop Charles Walmesley, a Benedictine monk and the vicar apostolic of England's western district, consecrated him bishop on August 15, 1790.

As bishop, Carroll dedicated himself to founding a fully vibrant Church for the new nation. He established parishes, founded a seminary, and invited various religious orders to enrich the fledgling Church with their prayers and good works: Sulpicians arrived to open and operate the seminary in Baltimore; Carmelites nuns established a first contemplative monastery for the new nation near the early Jesuit foundations in Port Tobacco, Maryland; Carroll laid the groundwork for the founding of the first Catholic girls school, which the Order of the Visitation opened under his successor; and he invited the Dominicans to establish missions for the growing Catholic population in Kentucky. Catholic population growth also inspired him to lay plans for the establishment of additional dioceses, which were executed in 1808 with new sees in Boston, New York, Philadelphia, and Bardstown, Kentucky. His devotion to the young Republic as his native land and its melting pot ideals was evident in both his undertakings and gestures: when a parish in Boston, the Church of the Holy Cross, split into rival French and Irish factions, he urged them to "lay aside national distinctions and attachments and strive to form not Irish or English or French congregations . . . but Catholic American congregations." Even his diocesan seal surrounded the Blessed Virgin not with the customary twelve stars but with thirteen, one each for the new nation's founding states.

Carroll was also open to a restoration of the Society of Jesus in the United States. There had been signals from Rome that Clement XIV's successors—Pius VI and Pius VII—desired a revival of the Society. Since the beginning of the Suppression, the ex-Jesuits in the United States had considered affiliating with the

Jesuits in Russia. Carroll was wary of that option: the Society had powerful enemies in Europe who were eager to see even the small remnant active in Russia destroyed, and any hint of insubordination would not serve the young American Church in Rome. Furthermore, a premature refounding of the Society might, he thought, permanently hobble what, if waited for, could constitute a more complete restoration of the order. An attempt to create a simulacrum of the old Society in the late 1790s further confused matters. This Society of the Faith of Jesus gained membership and a measure of patronage in Europe. Several ex-Jesuits in the United States looked into affiliating with it in 1800, though without success.

Decisions by Pius VII early in the 1800s allayed Carroll's concerns about a Russian affiliation. In the breve *Catholicae fidei* of 1801, Pius recognized the Jesuits in Russia as a province of the Society, permitted their superior to take the title superior general, and authorized him to admit members from outside Russia. Then the pope began tacitly approving the organization of Jesuits in Western European countries. In 1803 thirty-five ex-Jesuits reconstituted the English province at Stonyhurst, England, where the school once at Saint-Omer had relocated in 1794. Similar undertakings occurred in Sardinia, Parma, Naples, and Sicily. While civil authorities sometimes suppressed these provisional associations of Jesuits as quickly as they were founded, some managed to establish residences and restaff the occasional school and seminary, all with papal nods of approval.

Shortly after the reconstitution of the English province in 1803, Carroll forwarded to the superior general in Russia, Gabriel Gruber (1740–1805), a petition from multiple ex-Jesuits and others that requested their admission into the Society by aggregation with Russia. Carroll received Gruber's approval in 1805. Of the ten ex-Jesuits still alive in the United States, five renewed their vows in the summer and fall of 1805. Robert Molyneux (1738–1808), who had entered the order after studying at the College of Saint Omer in France before the Suppression, became their superior. The appointment of a first novice master fell to the pastor of Holy

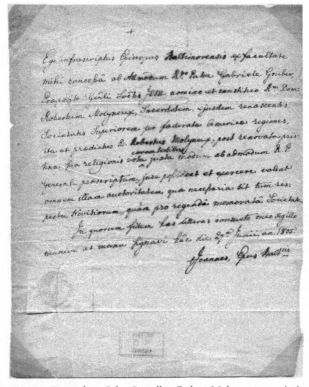

FIGURE 2.4   Letter from John Carroll to Robert Molyneux, appointing
Molyneux as superior of the American Jesuits, June 27, 1805: "I, the un-
dersigned bishop of Baltimore, with a faculty conceded to me by the Very
Reverend Father Gabriel Gruber, superior general of the Society of Jesus,
name and establish the Reverend Lord Robert Molyneux, a priest, superior of the same Society, now growing again, for the regions of the United
States. As a result thereof, and once he has renewed his previous vows of
religion before witnesses according to the manner prescribed by the Very
Reverend Father General, the aforementioned lord Robert Molyneux will
possess in law and validly exercise all that authority which is necessary as
much in respect to novices as for governing the aforementioned Society. In
guarantee of these things, I have secured this letter with my customary seal
and signed it by my hand on this 27th day of June, 1805. John, bishop of
Baltimore." Molyneux accepted the appointment on July 24 and renewed
his vows August 18 at Saint Ignatius Church, Port Tobacco, Maryland.
Source: Letter from John Carroll to Robert Molyneux, Appointment of
Rev. Molyneux as Superior of the American Jesuits, June 27, 1805, Maryland Province Archives, 119 2 4.

Trinity parish in Washington, Francis Neale (1756–1837), in 1806. Neale, a priest active in many ministries under Bishop Carroll's direction, had himself never entered the Society and so made the Spiritual Exercises for the first time with his novices. Advice was solicited from the novice master of the English Jesuits at Stonyhurst, Charles Plowden (1743–1821), who noted dryly in correspondence to Molyneux that Neale, never having been a Jesuit, "enter[ed] upon his office under a great disadvantage."

The first Jesuits from Russia began arriving almost immediately. Most were Western Europeans who had entered the Society and been trained at Polotsk and Daugavpils (now in Latvia). Soon the ranks of the US mission were filling with European Jesuits—first of the Russian Society, then from newly restored provinces across Europe—who saw in the young nation a land of great missionary promise and of reliable, if also startling, neutrality from civil authorities. A glance at two Jesuits sent from Russia and a third, sent briefly by the general superior, will highlight trends among Jesuits in the United States in the decades leading up to and after the universal restoration in 1814. A sign of the nomadic tendencies of this generation of Jesuits, all three of them returned to Europe, where they lived out their careers and died.

Anthony Kohlmann (1771–1836), an Alsatian, was among the first reinforcements to arrive in Maryland from Russia. Caught up in the turmoil of the French Revolution, Kohlmann studied for the priesthood at several seminaries, affiliated with multiple religious congregations, including the Capuchins, and was ordained a priest, before he entered the novitiate in Daugavpils in 1803. In 1806 he arrived in the United States in response to an appeal for missionaries. His first ministries were to German-speaking Catholics in Maryland and Pennsylvania. Kohlmann's general impressions of the reestablished Maryland mission were not positive. The rural orientation of Jesuit activity in the new mission was, as he saw it, thoughtlessly readopted from the colonial period. He was convinced that plantation culture sapped the Jesuits of manpower that would be better deployed elsewhere and accustomed the Jesuits to a way of life that was anathema to the order's true urban character. He was especially distressed at the mission's neglect of the new nation's burgeoning cities, especially given their growing Catholic populations. He saw the future of the Church in, above all other cities, New York. Kohlmann himself spent many years in New York, first as the administrator of the newly erected diocese, whose first bishop had been waylaid in Naples by the Napoleonic wars and died there in 1810. While standing in for the missing bishop, Kohlmann made two contributions of special significance, one to the general history of Catholicism in the United States, the other, more narrowly to the order's history. The former has to do with the seal of the confessional. Kohlmann came under legal scrutiny when he returned stolen property on behalf of a penitent and then refused to identify the penitent to authorities. Prosecutors indicted him for obstructing their investigations. The court, however, rejected the charge, holding that a priest cannot be obliged to violate the confidentiality of a sacramental confession. The legal precedent holds to the present day.

Kohlmann also founded a new school, the New York Literary Institute, on the site of the present day's Saint Patrick's Cathedral. By 1813 the school boasted seventy-four borders, both Catholic and Protestant. That very year, however, the Jesuit superior informed Kohlmann that the mission, consisting of only fifty Jesuits, did not have the manpower to support a school so far on its periphery. Kohlmann objected strenuously. He wrote to Rome that Maryland was "the poorest and most beggarly [state] of the whole union," and proposed that the facilities in Georgetown be redesignated a novitiate and the college faculty be moved to New York City. Kohlmann's petition was rejected, and Jesuits did not return to New York for another three decades. Kohlmann himself was brought back to Washington, to his certain distaste, where he simultaneously served as mission superior, Georgetown College rector, and professor of dogmatic theology. Kohlmann turned in 1820 to establish the Washington Seminary (now Gonzaga College High School) as a new novitiate and house of studies for Jesuits, which he pointedly located at the geographical and commercial heart of the city's federal district. That institution was transformed into a second college without boarding students to solve problems of space, enrollment, and financing at Georgetown in 1824. Given how unreliable plantation revenues were in these years, the school—in violation of the order's own rules—charged tuition. For precisely that reason, the general superior in Rome ordered the Jesuits to withdraw from the school in 1827. Local clergy tried to keep some vestige of it open, with limited success. On petition of Saint Louis University and Georgetown, the schools were permitted to charge tuition as of 1833. Still, the Maryland Jesuits did not return until 1848 to reopen the downtown school; and ten years later, it received a congressional charter as Gonzaga College.

These decades were a boom time for Jesuit colleges. Between 1840 and 1860 Jesuits founded or took over eighteen colleges nationwide. While Jesuits later closed or withdrew from some—for example, Saint Joseph's College in Saint Paul, Oregon, and the College of Saints Peter and Paul in Baton Rouge—most operate to the present day. Jesuits based in Saint Louis received a school from the bishop in Cincinnati in 1840 (now Saint Xavier High School and Xavier University). The Maryland Jesuits founded colleges in Philadelphia in 1851 (now Saint Joseph's Preparatory School and Saint Joseph's University), in Baltimore in 1852 (now Loyola-Blakefield Academy and Loyola University), and in Boston (now Boston College High School and Boston College) in 1858. French Jesuits in Louisiana founded the College of the Immaculate Conception in New Orleans (now Jesuit High School) in 1849. Their fellow countrymen moved from Kentucky in 1846 to take over the local bishop's Saint John's College in Westchester County (now Fordham Preparatory School and Fordham University in the Bronx), and from there in 1847 founded Xavier College (now Xavier High School) in Manhattan. Of the ten most populous cities in the United States in 1860, Buffalo and Brooklyn (not yet a borough of New York City) were the only cities without a Jesuit college. Of these two cities, the former gained a Jesuit school (now Canisius College) in 1870; and the latter, (Brooklyn College) in

1908. Alas, Kohlmann, who surely would have rejoiced at all these urban commitments, most especially in New York City, was not there to see any of it: he died in 1836 at the age of sixty-five in Rome, where he had been recalled to teach at the Pontifical Gregorian University, restored to the Society by Pope Leo XII in 1824.

Another European transplant from Russia to the United States was the Venetian Giovanni Antonio Grassi (1775–1849). Grassi entered the order in Russia in 1799. His superiors recognized an uncommon set of talents, both intellectual and administrative, and planned to send him to a mission in China. The Napoleonic wars impeded this plan. As he waited for the possibility of travel, he completed a course of studies in mathematics at Coimbra, Portugal, and in 1810 his superiors opted to send him to the United States. The rural tastes of the restored Jesuits baffled Grassi no less than Kohlmann, and the poor state of academic affairs at their principal institution, Georgetown College, disturbed him. He resolved to bring the curriculum into harmony with the standards of European colleges and invested in the college's infrastructure, most importantly the library. During his seven years as the school's president, he drew from his mathematical training and astronomical interests to make the college as vital a center of scientific investigation as could be managed. He also understood low enrollments to be at the heart of the school's financial stagnation and implemented a program of lowering fees to increase matriculation. His plan succeeded: as fees decreased, the student body increased, along with overall revenues.

Grassi was the superior who came into conflict with Kohlmann over the Literary Institute in New York. He had few allies in his strong stance against the school. Even Bishop Carroll expressed sympathy with shifting efforts to New York City. Grassi's determination had conflicting results: On the one hand, he left Georgetown College in better financial and academic shape than it had ever been. On the other hand, his decision to close the Literary Institute inspired an impatience toward the Maryland Jesuits that later encouraged New York bishop John Hughes to look anywhere else to staff Saint John's.

A third foreign-born Jesuit in the mission came for different purposes and under different circumstances. Dublin-born Peter Kenney (1779–1841) came not to join the mission but to reform it. He was a "visitor," an official in Jesuit law, who travels to particular regions to assess and solve problems that the local governance proves itself incapable of solving. The visitor acts as a plenipotentiary of the superior general in Rome. Kenney had entered the newly restored English province in 1804, made his novitiate at Stonyhurst, and completed his studies in Palermo. He returned to Ireland in 1811 to establish a new Jesuit province there and founded Clongowes Wood College outside Dublin in 1814.

Kenney served as a visitor to the United States twice: in 1819–21 and in 1830–33. The direction of the mission and the management of property were dominant problems during both visitations. The plantations, it will be recalled, had been the original source of financial support for the Jesuits in the colonial period. They were held in trust by Jesuits and their allies in the colonial period and were unified as the "Corporation of Roman Catholic Clergymen" in 1792 once Maryland developed its own corporation law after the Revolutionary War. With the restoration of the Society in the United States in 1805, control of the Corporation fell, but only gradually, to Jesuits. A problem then emerged: by law a corporation board elected its own new members, and Maryland corporation law required members to be US citizens. Yet the superior general appointed the governance of the mission, consisting of the mission superior and his council of advisers. These officials did not need to be US citizens, and many were not. The resulting incongruence between the mission leadership and the Corporation leadership led to conflict.

Three additional factors exacerbated this problem: First, management of the plantations led, as Kohlmann and others noted, to a drain on manpower from the growing urban works of the Society. Second, the plantations were not reliable generators of revenue and often required subsidies. And third, the first bishop of Baltimore with no previous affiliation with the Society of Jesus, Archbishop Ambrose Maréchal (r. 1817–28), argued that certain properties held by the Corporation properly belonged not to the Jesuits themselves but to the US Church and thus should be in the hands of the archbishops of Baltimore. Maréchal filed a claim to that effect with the Congregation for the Propagation of the Faith in 1821, and the dicastery seemed inclined to favor the archbishop's arguments.

Over the course of his two visitations, Kenney made decisions addressing these problems of governance and ownership. Regarding governance, with an eye to alleviating tensions between native- and foreign-born Jesuits and bringing the operation of the mission more in line with the overall interests of the Society, Kenney encouraged the mission to send promising scholastics to Europe for studies. He even selected the first four. In the 1820s and 1830s, these all assumed important leadership positions in the mission. Later, he also recommended the promotion of the Maryland mission to the status of province. The superior general, Jan Roothaan (1785–1853), elevated Maryland to a province in celebration of the mission's bicentennial in 1833. Regarding the property, Kenney compelled the Jesuit members of the Corporation to acknowledge that no decision should be made regarding the property that was not consonant with the mission superior's governance. He furthermore encouraged the improved management of the plantations and an overall distancing of the mission from the plantation operations, both in Maryland and in Missouri, where, newly arrived, Jesuits also held farmland.

A key moment in the process of distancing from the plantations counts as a terrible episode in American Jesuit history, namely, the disposition of the mission's slaves in the 1830s. Roman authorities never seem to have grasped how or why the American Jesuits were involved in the use of slave labor. Earlier experience with the Church's use of slave labor in South America, where the Jesuits claimed ownership of over 17,000 people in the mid–eighteenth century, did not provide Rome with an easy comparison. Now, after the Restoration, corporate Jesuit slaveholding was a peculiarity of North American Jesuits in the Maryland and Missouri missions (we will turn to the establishment of the latter mission in the next chapter) and at new French mission stations in the Mississippi and Ohio river valleys.

The early nineteenth-century debate between American Jesuits revolved primarily around the running of the farms in Maryland. When the enslaved labor was brought into discussion, the majority of the Jesuits, especially those born in America, favored keeping both the plantations and the enslaved people as part of the patrimony of the mission and with a condescending sense of moral obligation to care for the enslaved people. Although few Jesuits favored emancipation, in 1814 the leadership of the Corporation (then not yet in full Jesuit control, and sometimes at odds with the mission's Jesuit governance) resolved to emancipate the enslaved people in phases. They could continue to work as tenant farmers or perhaps instead go to Liberia, a strategy once proposed for all those of African descent by Thomas Jefferson. One local superior, Joseph Carbery (1784–1849), experimented with tenant farming at the southern-most Jesuit plantation, Saint Inigoes, Maryland; but his project garnered no larger support. In 1820, during Kenney's visitation to resolve the property conflicts, the 1814 decision of the Corporation was formally rescinded.

In the end, it was a third faction within the province whose plan won the day. Its principal concern was responsible investment. By these lights, the problem with the plantations was that they were not reliable sources of revenue for Jesuit enterprises. The Jesuits themselves produced a report that demonstrated slave labor was more expensive than hired labor. That insight might have pointed the province in the direction of Carbery's plan, but the Jesuits also saw the monetary value of the enslaved people themselves: their sale could provide revenue, which could be more profitably invested elsewhere. Banks were also emerging as better places for investment than land. Complicating matters was a growing fear in this period among slave owners, Jesuits included, that unrest among the enslaved might lead to a revolt and that abolitionist sentiment might force the slave owners to free the enslaved people without compensation.

FIGURE 2.5 Saint Thomas Manor / Saint Ignatius Church, Port Tobacco, Maryland, 1933. Despite architectural alteration over the centuries, still evident are the component parts of the manor house (on the right, 1741), a chapel (in the middle with the low roof, dating from 1697), and the church proper (on the left, 1798). The parish priests and their congregation were permitted to build the church after the disestablishment of the Anglican Church in Maryland's state constitution in 1776. Bishop John Carroll laid the cornerstone in 1798. The Jesuits had been active in the region since 1641, when Andrew White first attempted contact with local Potobac communities. Lord Baltimore granted the 4,000 acres around where the manor now stands to the Jesuits in 1649. Several former Jesuits renewed their vows in the church in the summer of 1805, marking the restoration of the Society in the United States. A financial assessment of Saint Thomas Manor in 1833 reported, "There are 45 [enslaved people] living on this land of whom nine are men or boys capable of work and seven women. The others are old persons and children." The photographer, John A. S. Brosnan (1860–1948), documented with photography much turn-of-the-twentieth-century Jesuit life in the Maryland–New York province. Source: Saint Thomas Manor / Saint Ignatius Church, Port Tobacco, Maryland, BFCSC, Woodstock Theological Library, Brosnan Photographic Collection, B0105-e002.

In the mid-1830s, two Jesuits who favored a sale-and-reinvestment solution held the most powerful positions in the newly formed province, the provincial superior and the rector of Georgetown College. When their terms expired, they exchanged offices. Along with other key members of the province, they persuaded the superior general in Rome to permit a mass sale. The sale was arranged with a prominent Louisiana politician and his business partner: 272 people for $115,000. The principal transfer of enslaved people in Maryland to Louisiana took place in 1838. The superior general had put several conditions on the sale, including that the sale revenues be used for endowments, in particular for the training of young Jesuits, and in any event not for operating expenses or paying off debts. When the down payment of $25,000 arrived, the provincial, Thomas F. Mulledy (1794–1860), used $8,000 to settle the conflict with the archbishops of Baltimore with a contribution to their pension fund and $17,000 to relieve debt he had accrued through building projects at Georgetown College.

Outrage at the sale and the misuse of the down payment among the divided Maryland Jesuits ensued. It was exacerbated by reports from Louisiana that enslaved families were being separated and the baptized slaves were being deprived of Catholic religious services, two additional issues on which the superior general had given instruction. In consequence, the provincial resigned and rushed to Rome to plead his case directly. He remained there for two years while others worked to put the province back on track. In the meantime, the plantations converted to tenant labor. Concluding words on this episode we leave to the eminent twentieth-century historian of African American Catholicism, Cyprian Davis, OSB: "The tragic story of the Jesuit slaves presents to us not only the harshness of slavery as it really existed but also the moral quicksand of expediency and inhumanity that sooner or later trapped everyone who participated in the ownership and buying and selling of human beings."

While the four decades of the Society's universal suppression were of obvious significance to it, they had a very particular way of playing out in the United States, and they were of defining importance for Catholicism in America. By leaving the priests in place and without an alternate structure to which to submit, the Suppression forced the emergence of a new, local Church aspiring to all the characteristics of a self-sufficient Church. By the time a new Jesuit mission was established in Maryland, this national Church was self-sufficient enough that the returning Jesuits could focus on the matters particularly suited to it, especially education.

From this perspective, the domestic restoration of 1805 is a decisive moment in US Jesuit history, and in key respects more so than the universal restoration of 1814. Questions and challenges emerged in that decade between the local and the universal restorations that oriented Jesuit activities on the East Coast and across the new nation for generations to come: whether to move beyond the mission's regional origins, and how; whether to move into cities, and which ones; whether to rely on the plantations, and how to fund new projects; whether to found schools, and what kinds; and whether to serve the new waves of Catholic immigrant population, and how. This is not to suggest that the Restoration of 1814 had no effect, but its most important effects had mainly to do with the ways that the Restoration was received not in the United States but in Europe. That reaction, a negative one in many circles, explains why and how in the nineteenth century so many European Jesuits ended up in the United States. In this regard, four national groups are decisive to understanding the history of the Jesuits in the nineteenth-century United States: the Belgians, the Italians, the Germans, and the French. We examine them in our next chapter.

Further Reading

Primary Literature

Georgetown's Second Founder: Fr. Giovanni Grassi's News on the Present Condition of the Republic of the United States of North America. Roberto Severino, trans. Washington, DC: Georgetown University

Press, 2021. Grassi served in the Maryland mission from 1810 until 1817, including a tenure as Georgetown College president, during which he greatly modernized the curriculum and the student body grew. Shortly after his return to Turin, he penned these Tocquevillesque observations of the young nation and Catholicism in it.

Hanley, Thomas O'Brien, ed. *The John Carroll Papers*. Notre Dame, IN: University of Notre Dame Press, 1976. This monumental undertaking, sponsored by the American Catholic Historical Society, comprises Carroll's writings as a student in Europe, a young priest, and the nation's first Catholic bishop. Writings that were originally in Latin and French appear in translation.

Rothman, Adam, and Elsa Barraza Mendoza, eds. *Facing Georgetown's History: A Reader on Slavery, Memory, and Reconciliation*. Washington, DC: Georgetown University Press, 2021. The history of Jesuit slaveholding in the United States has attracted considerable national attention in recent years. Georgetown University's handling of the history and its implications opened the way for a robust Jesuit engagement with this history. This volume presents key documents both from the history of Jesuit slaveholding on the East Coast in the colonial and early national periods and from the ongoing initiatives that involve the descendants of those enslaved by Jesuits, the university, and the Jesuit order itself.

Secondary Literature

Buckley, Cornelius M. *Stephen Larigaudelle Dubuisson, SJ (1786–1864) and the Reform of the American Jesuits*. Lanham, MD: University Press of America, 2013. Dubuisson was an unusual, intriguing, and influential figure in the early nineteenth-century reemergence of the Society in the United States. He was a celebrated, and sometimes controversial, pastor in the mid-Atlantic states for a decade before he was sent to Rome in 1826. There he became a trusted, informal counselor to superiors general on all matters American. His inclinations were ultramontane, and he advised accordingly. He thus represents, and colorfully so, one strategy to the fundamental challenge the Jesuits have faced throughout their American history over how best to adapt a universal vision to local circumstance.

Morrissey, Thomas J. *Peter Kenney, SJ, 1779–1841: The Restoration of the Jesuits in Ireland, England, Sicily, and North America.* Washington, DC: Catholic University of America Press, 2014. Thanks to his two official visits to US Jesuits on behalf of the order's superior general in the early nineteenth century, the Irish Jesuit Peter Kenney ranks with John Carroll himself as among the most important figures in the history of the Restoration and for the trajectory taken in that century by the order.

———

The following volumes, most of which are collections of chapters from historians of diverse specializations, appreciate the Suppression and Restoration as processes that shared certain underlying inspirations but that also unfolded in distinct ways around the world. The edited volumes touch at least in part on those processes as they expressly shaped the experience of Jesuits and the Church, either in the Thirteen Colonies (at the Suppression) or in the United States (by the period of restoration). Two of the three monographs (*Reform Catholicism* and *English Jesuit Education*) address issues beyond the Maryland mission proper but with significant implications for it.

Burson, Jeffrey D., and Jonathan Wright, eds. *The Jesuit Suppression in Global Context: Causes, Events, and Consequences.* Cambridge: Cambridge University Press, 2015. A collection of essays examining the Suppression, as the title suggests, in global context.

Maryks, Robert A., and Jonathan Wright, eds. *Jesuit Survival and Restoration: A Global History, 1773–1900.* Leiden: Brill, 2014. This volume includes interesting and relevant chapters on the Society in Russia, the order's corporate survival in England during the Suppression, the struggle for universal restoration after 1814, John Carroll's activities in the United States, and the return of Jesuits to Canada.

McCoog, Thomas M., ed. *"Promising Hope": Essays on the Suppression and Restoration of the English Province of the Society of Jesus.* Rome: Institutum Historicum Societatis Iesu, 2003. A collection of previously published articles focused on the activities of former Jesuits in England and Ireland. Several chapters touch also on former Jesuits' activities in the United States.

Van Kley, Dale K. *Reform Catholicism and the International Suppression of the Jesuits in Enlightenment Europe.* New Haven, CT: Yale University Press, 2018. The eminent historian Dale Van Kley redirects attention in this history of the Suppression from one cause usually blamed for it, the secular Enlightenment, to another, what Van Kley calls "Reform Catholicism," which favored a more decentralized, more nationalized Catholicism and saw in the Jesuits its most dangerous opponent.

Whitehead, Maurice. *English Jesuit Education: Expulsion, Suppression, Survival, Restoration, 1762–1803.* Burlington, VT: Ashgate, 2013. This work traces the survival of educational establishments founded by the Jesuits through the Suppression, the French Revolution, and the Restoration. It highlights the activities of English Jesuits in the emergent restored Maryland mission as well.

3

Haven, 1821–1900

THE UNIVERSAL RESTORATION of the Society of Jesus through Pope Pius VII's *Sollicitudo omnium ecclesiarum* inspired a range of reactions within the United States. When word reached Washington in 1814, the rector of George-town College, the Jesuit father Giovanni Antonio Grassi, con-vened the students and faculty to sing a *Te Deum*, after which they returned to their classes. Two American Founding Fathers, however, reacted ominously. John Adams wrote to Thomas Jefferson in 1816:

> I do not like the late resurrection of the Jesuits. Shall we not have swarms of them here, in as many shapes and disguises as ever a king of Gypsies, . . . himself assumed? If . . . any con-gregation of men could merit eternal perdition on earth and in hell, . . . it is this company of Loyola. . . . Our system . . . of religious liberty might oblige us to afford them an asylum. . . . But if they do not put the purity of our elections to a severe trial, it will be a wonder.

Jefferson agreed: "Their restoration . . . makes a retrograde step from light towards darkness."

The divergent reactions raise the question of what exactly was "restored" as a result of *Sollicitudo*. On the one hand, Grassi's restrained reaction reflects something true in the United States that was true really nowhere else in the world: when word of the Restoration reached him, the mission had been developing for nearly a decade and was already larger, at some fifty Jesuits, and more widely geographically distributed along the East Coast than its predecessor before the Suppression had ever been. In that respect, *Sollicitudo* promised to the rest of the world what was already to be found in the United States. On the other hand, Adams's words proved prescient in their own way: Jesuits did, in fact, swarm to the United States. While *Sollicitudo* allowed in Church law for the reopening of novitiates and the growth of the order across Europe, a new hostility toward the Jesuits from an emergent anticlerical ruling elite drove them out of it. Anti-Catholicism found fertile soil in the new republic as well, but the constitutionally protected religious liberty Adams described let these Jesuits in nonetheless. The tremendous potential for religious work in America drew them there. Most nineteenth-century immigrant Jesuits worked with the growing Catholic immigrant population, and the mission to Native Americans remained tremendously appealing. Setting the tone in Rome was Jan Roothaan, the second superior general of the restored Society (r. 1829–53), who was encouraging Jesuits to recover the spirituality of the original Society, to reestablish their global presence in the missions, and to regain the order's educational eminence.

With these needs on the ground and encouragements from Rome, the Jesuit refugees to the United States were of four main national groups, which tended to orient their activities within particular geographical regions: Belgian Jesuits established a base of operation in Saint Louis from which they moved north along the Mississippi River and into the Indian territories of the northwest; Italians moved into the Rocky Mountains and beyond to the Pacific Coast, where they established, first, Native American missions and then schools for white settlers; Germans scattered first around the Great Lakes and then onto the Great Plains to work with German immigrants and Native peoples; and the French returned to a corridor from Quebec to New Orleans. This chapter examines the arrival and progress of these four groups over the course of the nineteenth century.

BELGIAN JESUITS

Two non-Jesuits are at the origins of the Belgian history in the American Midwest. The first is Charles Nerinckx, a diocesan priest from Mechelen whom Bishop Carroll recruited to Kentucky in 1804. In 1816, on the way to Rome to gain the approval of a constitution for a congregation of sisters he had founded, the Sisters of Loretto, he stopped at his old seminary outside Brussels. An article he had written about Kentucky stirred up interest at the seminary and inspired ten seminarians to accompany him back to the United States. After arriving in Baltimore, six remained to enter the Jesuit novitiate at Georgetown College.

On a second trip to the Low Countries, Nerinckx attracted another eleven recruits for the Maryland mission. Anticlerical laws recently imposed by King William I prohibited Jesuits from his realm and so helped Nericnkx's recruiting efforts. Although Belgians in exile could enter a novitiate in Switzerland, it was not clear how long before the Swiss, too, would expel the order. Upon arriving in the United States in 1821, these next recruits attended the novitiate in White Marsh outside Washington. The financial state of the Maryland mission, however, was precarious, and the mission superior, Charles Neale, was considering closing the novitiate altogether. At about the same time, the bishop of Louisiana and the Two Floridas (a diocese covering the Florida Peninsula, the northern Gulf Coast territory, and much of the Louisiana Territory) petitioned the Jesuits to take up residence near Saint Louis on the Mississippi River and to work with Native American communities in the vicinity. That bishop, Louis-Guillaume Dubourg, was a Sulpician father and the second non-Jesuit who played a part in the Belgians arriving in the Midwest. Dubourg knew the Maryland Jesuits well. He had arrived in Baltimore in 1793, a refugee from the French Revolution. Bishop Carroll recruited him, with other Sulpicians, to staff Georgetown

College. Dubourg served as the school's president from 1796 to 1799, and then as president of Saint Mary's Seminary in Baltimore for the next thirteen years. He was elevated to the bishopric of Louisiana and the Two Floridas in 1818.

Neale accepted Dubourg's request by sending the entire novitiate from White Marsh to the Florissant Valley, outside Saint Louis. The novice master, Charles Van Quickenborne (1788–1837), with his assistant, ten novices, and six enslaved people, made the trip in four and a half weeks in the spring of 1823. When they arrived, as legend has it, Sacred Heart Sister Rose Philippine Duchesne welcomed them with an apple pie, which the austere novice master declined as an extravagance. In addition to the novitiate, the Jesuits founded a school for Native American boys, the Saint Regis Seminary. Farming revenues supported the Jesuits here, as in Maryland. Another early source of income was the US Department of War, which was responsible for controlling the Native populations in the interest of white settlers' westward expansion. The department secretary, John C. Calhoun, offered an annual stipend of $200 per priest for work on such missions. He wrote Dubourg: "The establishment of a school on the principles which you have suggested is much better calculated to effect your benevolent design of extending the benefits of civilization to the remote tribes, and with it, the just influence of the government."

In 1828 Dubourg's successor handed over Saint Louis College (now Saint Louis High School and Saint Louis University), founded with diocesan clergy in 1818, to the Jesuits. The school received a civil charter as a university in 1832, but its struggles to develop professional schools exemplify recurrent challenges Jesuit educators faced in the nineteenth century. For example, Saint Louis' medical department, founded in 1836, awarded the first medical degree west of the Mississippi River in 1839, but anti-Catholic activism made its separation from the university a requirement for its survival in 1854. The medical faculty affiliated with the nondenominational Washington University in Saint Louis at the end of the century and remains so to this day. The university's faculty of law, also the first in the American West, lasted only four years. When its charismatic founding dean died in 1847, the university's chronicler noted that "the Law School was buried with him." Only in the very different educational context of the early twentieth century were law and medical departments again able to be part of the Jesuits' educational program at Saint Louis.

In contrast to the professional schools, the colleges of the Missouri mission (made independent of Maryland and placed directly under the superior general in 1831) grew into a strong educational network covering the Mississippi River watershed. "College," in this context, is an umbrella term. In its fullest form, it encompassed a seven-year program divided between lower and upper schools and straddling what would today be called high school and college. Often it offered only part of that program. Sometimes Jesuit colleges provided for boarders; sometimes not. Sometimes Jesuits founded colleges on their own initiative or at the invitation of a local bishop; sometimes Jesuits were offered schools already in operation. Examples of all these variations emerged in both the Maryland and Missouri missions.

Jesuit expansion into education relied heavily on the encouragement of local bishops and major donors. The bishop of Cincinnati placed his school, the Athenaeum, into the care of Jesuits in 1840, who renamed it Xavier College. In Chicago the bishop offered the Jesuits a parish and insisted that an eloquent young Jesuit, the Dutch-born Arnold Damen (1815–90), whom he knew from his time in Saint Louis, be charged with founding it. Damen had arrived at Florissant, Missouri, in 1837, drawn by missionaries' tales of the American West. As word of the Jesuits' arrival in Chicago spread, the local paper, the *Tribune*, urged the city's Protestant elite to "think twice before aiding . . . the founding of Jesuit institutions in this city. . . . The Society of Jesus is the most virulent and relentless enemy of the Protestant faith and Democratic government." Despite the paper's opposition, Damen ceremonially laid the cornerstone of Holy Name Church in 1857. It was another dozen years before the college opened. The lower school, now Saint Ignatius College Preparatory School, still occupies the original site; the upper school, now Loyola University, established a larger campus for itself on the North Side of the city in 1912.

The bishop of Detroit, an alumnus of the college in Cincinnati, was eager for a college in his own diocese. John Baptist Miège (1815–84) arrived to found one in 1877. A refugee from conflict on the Italian Peninsula, Miège had been consecrated a bishop to serve as vicar apostolic for the Indian Territories, built its cathedral in Leavenworth, directed the founding of dozens of parish grammar schools, attended the First Vatican Council (1869–70), and undertook a fund-raising mission to South America. He was three years into his retirement when his Jesuit superiors sent him to found the college in Detroit. Another bishop's invitation brought the Jesuits to Omaha in 1878. Roman Shaffel (1838–1908) was at Saint Ignatius College in Chicago when he was called along with five confreres to start this new foundation, which took the family name of the donor's husband, a local rancher and banker, Edward Creighton.

The final nineteenth-century academic foundation of the Missouri province (a vice province as of 1841, and the second province in the United States as of 1863) was in Wisconsin. With monies received from Belgian benefactors seven years earlier, the local bishop offered the Jesuits a parish in Milwaukee in 1855, hoping that the Jesuits would soon also found a school. Two years later the Jesuits opened Saint Aloysius Academy. The bishop acquired additional property for the school and a legal charter for a college in 1864. The college opened under the name of the famed seventeenth-century French Jesuit explorer Jacques Marquette (1637–75) in 1881. All these colleges were founded for the European Catholic immigrant population. The Jesuits used the colleges as home bases for a wide range of apostolic engagements in addition to educational ones, and most colleges were also paired with parishes.

West of the Mississippi, another great project was simultaneously taking shape. Although the distance from Native American populations hindered the recruitment of students to the Saint Regis Seminary outside Saint Louis, the school became the launching pad for an expanding network of mission stations to Native peoples in the continental high plains. Pierre-Jean De Smet (1801–73), who had been among Nerinckx's second group of Belgian recruits and who had traveled as a novice from White Marsh to Florissant in 1823, pioneered this enterprise. In 1838 and 1839, De Smet, alongside Billy Caldwell, an Irish–Native American leader of a Potawatomi community, helped to establish Saint Joseph's Mission, some three hundred miles northwest of Saint Louis at what is now Council Bluffs, Iowa. These Native Americans were refugees from Illinois and had settled in the abandoned blockhouse of a decommissioned US army fort. Further to the northwest, Iroquois refugees had introduced Flatheads, themselves refugees in the Valley of the Ootlashoots (Bitterroot, Montana), to Christianity. These communities became determined to recruit "Blackrobes," as they called the Jesuits, to their territory. Multiple delegations headed to Saint Louis in the 1830s with that hope. At the same time, the US bishops formally recommended to Pope Gregory XIV in 1833 that the missions to Native Americans be entrusted to the Society of Jesus, and the superior general in Rome subsequently accepted the charge. Finally, in 1840, superiors permitted De Smet to head deeper into Indian territories with a team from the American Fur Company. This arrangement was reminiscent of the earlier Jesuit voyages with fur traders in New France—and the goal of the self-sustaining, geographically isolated communities Jesuits had founded in South America. The aim of these settlements, known as reductions, was to protect Indigenous peoples from certain kinds of white exploitation while at the same time encouraging their Christianization and assimilation into Western society. In these respects, the Jesuits' interests and the government's interests, as since Calhoun's early support for Dubourg's missions, coincided.

De Smet moved quickly. In less than a quarter century, he founded eighteen missions between Saint Louis and the southwest corner of Canada. Developing and sustaining the missions fell to other Jesuits. De Smet traveled across the Atlantic nineteen times, and logged as many as 260,000 miles, on foot, on horseback, and

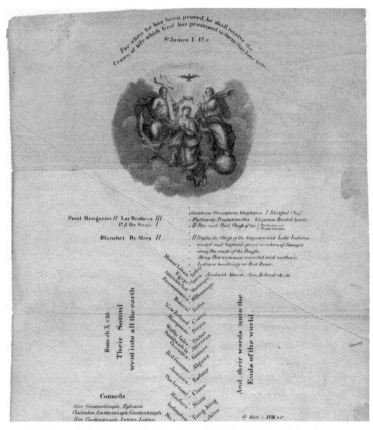

FIGURE 3.1   Symbolic Catechism (detail), 1843. A "Catholic Ladder" consists of images and small blocks of text in a vertical sequence to indicate pathways to Heaven. In this upper segment of a "Catholic Ladder," designed by Pierre-Jean De Smet, the adoption of Christianity by named Native peoples appears on the trajectory of Christian salvation history. Source: Symbolic Catechism, 1843, Marquette University Archives, Milwaukee, Bureau of Catholic Indian Missions, ID MUA ITS 00035.

by boat, ship, and train. He was an energetic fundraiser for the missions. He recruited many personnel—men and women, including other religious orders—to the missions. He wrote innumerable reports. He mapped and illustrated, along with Father Nicolas Point (1799–1868), the geography, which was new and unknown

FIGURE 3.2   De Smet with chiefs at Fort Vancouver, 1859. As General George Wright's brutal prosecution of a war of retaliation against Plateau tribes drew to a close in 1858, the secretary of war solicited De Smet's help in arranging peace. De Smet traveled 1,600 miles on horseback over six months in Indian territory to assess the situation and then accompanied the chiefs to Fort Vancouver for peace talks, where this daguerreotype was made. An army adjutant in attendance described the priest's role afterward: "By the campaign of last summer submission had been conquered, but the embittered feelings of the two races, excited by war, still existed, and it remained for [De Smet] to supply that which was wanting to the sword. It was necessary to exercise the strong faith which the red man possessed in [his] purity and holiness of character; . . . the victory is [his]." Seated (left to right): Victor Happy-Man, Kalispel; Alexander Man-without-a-Horse, Pend Oreille; Adolphe Red-Feather, Flathead; Andrew Seppline, Coeur d'Alene. Standing: Denis Thunders-Robe, Colville; Bonaventure, Coeur d'Alene; Pierre De Smet; Francis Xavier, Flathead. Source: De Smet with chiefs at Fort Vancouver, 1859, Jesuit Archives and Research Center, Saint Louis (hereafter, JARC), Missouri Province Archives, De Smetiana IX-L2-A.

to whites. While his fast pace led to grumbling among the Jesuits left behind to sustain the many new foundations, he earned the respect of Native American leaders and government officials alike as a negotiator during the late nineteenth-century wars between the Native Americans and the US. In one legendary instance,

the Lakota chief Sitting Bull, having rejected the Treaty of Fort
Laramie at the end of Red Cloud's War (1866–68) over territory
in Montana, agreed to meet with De Smet to minimize further
bloodshed. As it turned out, the federal government did not honor
the terms of the treaty for long, and open war broke out again in
1876. This time, the government simply annexed the Montana
territories that treaties had granted to Native Americans in 1868.

ITALIAN JESUITS: THREE WAVES, THREE WORKS

De Smet was also instrumental in getting Italian Jesuits into the
Indian territories. But the story of the Italians in America began
earlier. Several Italian Jesuits had even arrived before the full restoration of the Society, for example, Giovanni Grassi. But Italian
Jesuits came in waves after *Sollicitudo* in consequence of the nationalist wars on the Italian Peninsula. They made three major
contributions to the Jesuit presence in the United States: they
augmented the number of Jesuits across North America, especially in the western Indian territories; they encouraged greater
conformity among the American Jesuits to European standards
of religious life; and they increased the number of educational
institutions, especially in the West.

Their first effect was simply to enhance the manpower of the
beleaguered Maryland Province. In 1848 the Maryland Province
consisted of forty-five priests, thirty-six scholastics, and sixty-four
brothers, assigned to eighteen houses and including four colleges
(two, Georgetown and the College of the Holy Cross in Massachusetts, with boarders; two more, Saint John's in Frederick, Maryland, (now Saint John's Catholic Preparatory School in Buckeystown, and no longer affiliated with the order, and the Washington
Seminary, with no boarding facilities) and mission churches from
Saint Inigoe's in southern Maryland to Old Town in Maine. Jesuits
began arriving that year from Rome in numbers and took an immediate interest in the educational enterprises they found. Italian
surnames became ever more common among the faculty and

administration of the schools; and the colleges rallied to recruit larger student bodies, now more easily served by the larger faculties. The Italians had a striking effect on science curricula. Several accomplished Italian Jesuit scientists took up residence at Jesuit colleges in the United States. The most notable example, Angelo Secchi (1818–78), briefly resided at Georgetown College to study theology and work at the college's observatory. Many years later he became recognized as a father of astrophysics for his work on astral spectroscopy.

By the mid-1850s, the turmoil in Rome seemed to have settled, and many Italians returned home. New expulsions from the Piedmont region, however, kept the overall number of Italian Jesuits in the United States on the increase. Like nearly all immigrant Jesuits since the Restoration, the Piedmontese were frustrated by the rural proclivities of the American Jesuits. But where the Romans seemed satisfied with the idea that their good example might persuade the Americans to their own improvement, the Piedmontese began writing to superiors in Rome. They complained about the excessive number of parishes, the abundance of activities in farm country, and all aspects of the American Jesuits' "common life," including their tendency to vacation alone and to receive visitors "at every hour of day and night." Furthermore, the Piedmontese reported to Rome that American novices were not fulfilling standard requirements of the novitiate, and the philosophical and theological training for Jesuits-in-training was woefully substandard. The very observatory in which Secchi and his confrere Benedict Sestini (1816–90) engaged in research had been built by a provincial who had seemingly misread Roothaan's denial of permission, in Latin, to build an observatory in the first place.

These complaints led to the appointment of another visitor, the Roman Jesuit Felice Sopranis (1799–1876) in 1859. Rome saw Sopranis as the perfect man to bring the wayward Americans into line: he was both reliable in his understanding of religious life and familiar with American ways, having taken refuge in Boston from Italian anticlerical violence in 1848. In the four years of his tenure, he traveled from Nova Scotia to the San Francisco Bay. During the visitation, he appointed the Neapolitan Angelo Paresce (1817–79) as the new provincial of Maryland. Prompted by Sopranis's concerns about Jesuits' theological training, Paresce began the task of establishing a new, national theology faculty. The school was founded in the small town of Woodstock outside of Baltimore. The choice of this rural location was controversial from the outset. Paresce, who rejected several sites closer to Baltimore, was convinced, wrongly as it turned out, that the 20-mile distance would soon be covered with trolley lines.

The school opened in the fall of 1869, and the faculty was largely Neapolitan. That province, whose members constituted the third wave of Italian refugee Jesuits to the US, had negotiated free tuition for their scholastics in return for sending their theologians to Woodstock. Paresce, as rector, led the faculty with Camillo Mazzella (1833–1900) as the prefect of studies. Mazzella became esteemed, even beloved, among American Jesuits: He took the unusual step of becoming a naturalized US citizen, served as the superior general's visitor to the Neapolitan province's New Mexico mission in 1875, was recalled to Rome in 1878 to teach theology at the Jesuits' Gregorian University, and became a strong proponent of the late nineteenth-century Thomistic renewal. Leo XIII created him a cardinal in 1886. Paresce's successor as provincial, Joseph Keller (1827–86), later enthused, with reference to an anticlerical Italian nationalist general: "God alone can repay the province of Naples. . . . Thanks be to God and Garibaldi. . . . Without Naples we would still be doing our ABCs."

Woodstock College not only met its goal of providing scholastics with sound theological training but also established itself as a command post for Catholic theology in the nation. It opened, for example, a printing house that produced an abundance of Catholic literature, including the household periodical *The Sacred Heart Messenger*, and *The Woodstock Letters*, a collection of reports, studies, essays, and opinion pieces, written as a repository of information for Jesuits about the works they were engaged in and the state of the Church and the Society around the globe. In matters of theology, the faculty itself inclined toward strong support of the pope, especially in the wake of Vatican Council I. Under Mazzella, the faculty embraced the Thomistic renewal as developed by such European Jesuits as Matteo Liberatore (1810–92) and Josef Kleutgen (1811–83) and endorsed by Pope Leo XIII in the encyclical *Aeterni Patris* in 1879. When Leo condemned Americanism, a set of largely stylized ideas supportive of the separation of church and state and the freedom of individual conscience in matters of religion, the theologians at Woodstock rallied in his support. At the same time, the US Jesuits gave little sign of abandoning their alliance with the liberal ideals that had welcomed them in the colonial period and propped open the Republic's door to Catholics, however reluctantly, as the European variety of liberalism persecuted them. Nor can one find in reaction to Leo's condemnation a strategic realignment in how the Jesuits ran their schools or operated their missions. In short, the Jesuits, as a group, struggled to embrace both papal anti-Modernism and American liberalism, despite their obvious contradictions. Retreat to an anti-Modernist Catholic ghetto was outside the bounds of their corporate imagination in the nineteenth century, as it had been up to the Suppression.

Italians in Indian Territories

The second major enterprise of Italian Jesuits was the Indian missions in the continental West. Returning from a fund-raising visit to Europe in 1844 with five recruits, De Smet introduced Giovanni Nobili (1812–56) to the mission in the Rocky Mountains. Nobili progressed on his own into the Oregon Territory, where he traveled between and worked at mission stations, most of which De Smet himself had founded during earlier travels. In 1849 Nobili and fellow Italian Michael Accolti (1807–78) traveled south into the California Territory, where the bishop of Monterey persuaded them to accept the Santa Clara mission church. Nobili established a college there in 1851 (now Santa Clara University), which expanded like so many similar foundations to serve the immigrant European population. As short on personnel as it was on money,

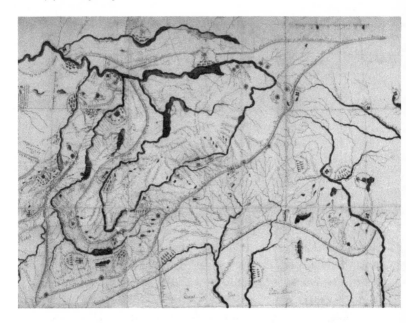

FIGURE 3.3 Map of the Northern Rocky Mountains and Plateau—detail. The map dates between 1842 and 1848. The map plots villages, missions, forts, trails, rivers and their tributaries, and mountain ranges. Giovanni Nobili (1812–56), whose name appears in a corner of the map, accompanied De Smet on travels in the Rocky Mountains and Oregon Territory, established and maintained multiple mission stations in the Rocky Mountain Mission of the Turin Province, and founded a college at the Santa Clara mission in California in 1851. Source: Map of the Northern Rocky Mountains and Plateau, JARC, Missouri Province Archives, De Smetiana, IX-C8-13.

Nobili strategically arranged to be in Rome in July 1853, just as a general congregation—a meeting of Jesuit delegates from around the globe—was convening. There, he persuaded the Turin province, in exile on account of the nationalist wars in Piedmont, to take over the Rocky Mountain mission. And so the Piedmontese, who had been operating in Corsica and Monaco, turned to the schools in California and the Indian missions in Oregon. Fresh Italian recruits founded new colleges in San Francisco (1855; now Saint Ignatius Preparatory School and the University of

San Francisco) and later Seattle (1891; now Seattle Preparatory School and Seattle University). Additional Italian personnel started arriving by way of Spain in the 1860s, and they expanded the mission's outreach to the Spanish-speaking population in the American Southwest.

In a region falling today in the state of Idaho, the Coeur d'Alene mission was proving a vital center of Jesuit activity. De Smet encountered the Coeur d'Alene tribe for the first time on his way back to the Saint Mary's Mission in Montana in 1842. Unable to stay, he promised to send confreres back. Antonio Ravalli (1812–84), recruited to the United States with Nobili and Accolti, took up residence in 1850. Under his leadership the mission became a flourishing settlement that included communal gardens, pastures, and livestock to support its inhabitants. The missionaries negotiated as best they could with local government officials to protect the Coeur d'Alene from the burgeoning white settler population.

The Coeur d'Alene mission became a home base for Jesuits reaching out to other tribes in the region. From there, the Sicilian Jesuit Giuseppe Cataldo (1837–1928) developed contact begun by De Smet with another tribe, the Spokane. He built a chapel by falls in the Spokane River 45 miles east of its confluence with the Columbia River. Cataldo, a refugee from Garibaldi's expulsion of the Jesuits in 1860, had come to the Rocky Mountain mission in answer to the visitor Sopranis's call for reinforcements. Cataldo had a gift for Native American languages and learned close to twenty. He began teaching children hymns and prayers, which gradually attracted their parents to the chapel.

The goal of these Jesuit missions was indeed the conversion of Native Americans to Christianity and their assimilation into mainstream Western society. Even as the Jesuits were complicit in the larger US strategy of suppressing Native society and culture, their missionary strategy was in certain respects more accommodationist, a style developed by the Jesuits centuries earlier and evident now in this nineteenth-century Italian mission. Accommodationism simply meant that the Jesuits were flexible in accepting and adapting to aspects of Indigenous cultures that more rigorist missionaries might reject. Baptism, for example, tended to be a more immediately pressing goal for many Protestant preachers. Jesuits were prepared to wait years, even decades, for formal conversion; and in the meantime they built infrastructure into their missions—schools, churches, and other civic buildings—and encouraged cultivation of the land. The wife of a government agent to the tribes of western Montana wrote: "It was [the Jesuits'] custom to adopt whatever they could of the Indians' own to the observing and celebrating of religious rites." While Jesuits did found boarding schools, which not only educated and trained Native children but also separated children from their parents and worked to suppress Native language and culture, Jesuits tended to found their schools on each reservation, rather than the common practice of establishing centralized boarding schools for children far from their homes. Jesuits, themselves being so often foreign, had a less rigid notion of what aspects of American culture were essential for the Native Americans to adopt. Even the English language was more foreign to some missionaries than to many Natives.

The Jesuits established a formal mission to the Spokane in 1878 and promised at least one Jesuit for the winter months. Cataldo, now the superior of the Rocky Mountain Mission, purchased two plots in the area in 1881, one for a larger chapel, the other for a future school. He invited the Canadian Sisters of Providence to staff a hospital in the city of Spokane. In the last decade of the nineteenth century, the white population in the region increased due to industrial developments such as the Northwest Rail and valuable mineral discoveries in mountainous Indian territories in and around Coeur d'Alene. Tensions between whites and Native Americans led the government to offer the Spokane a reservation, which the tribe refused. The Jesuits instead encouraged the Spokane to resettle on the Flathead and Coeur d'Alene reservations. With a declining Native population and an increasing settler population, the Jesuits reduced their commitment to the mission and increased their service to the settlers. A further sign of the racial tensions the Jesuit were required to negotiate: despite Cataldo's initial hope that the school would become part of the Jesuits' outreach to Native communities and an adequate Catholic rival to Protestant missions, the college that opened under the patronage of Saint Aloysius Gonzaga in 1887 (now Gonzaga Preparatory School and Gonzaga University) was, by contract with the city, restricted to white students.

Another group of exiled Neapolitan Jesuits worked in what became known as the Colorado–New Mexico Mission. Their first foundation was a small college in a region of the territory known as Las Vegas in 1877, a modestly developed area along a much older trade route connecting northern New Mexico and southern California (and not related to the notorious gambling resort established in Nevada in 1905). The school attracted 130 students in its first year but struggled against the anti-Catholic prejudice of the governor, who refused to sign its articles of incorporation, explaining that the Society "has been denounced time and again by the head of the Catholic Church, and justly expelled from the most enlightened countries of Europe." A debate ensued in Washington over the authority of a territorial government to certify such charters in the first place. Eight years later, another school was founded in Morrison, Colorado, under the name College of the Sacred Heart. In 1887 the colleges in Las Vegas and Morrison were closed and the faculties merged into a new college, built in Denver and named Regis College (now Regis Jesuit High School and Regis University) in 1921.

FRENCH JESUITS

After new anticlerical legislation was inspired by the July Revolution of 1830, French Jesuits began returning in numbers to the Mississippi and Ohio river valleys. In the case of Kentucky, we see at once the importance of the Society's relationship to bishops but also the tricky choices such relationships required them to make. The Sulpician bishop of Bardstown, Benedict Joseph Flaget, who had sent Nerinckx to Belgium to recruit priests for the

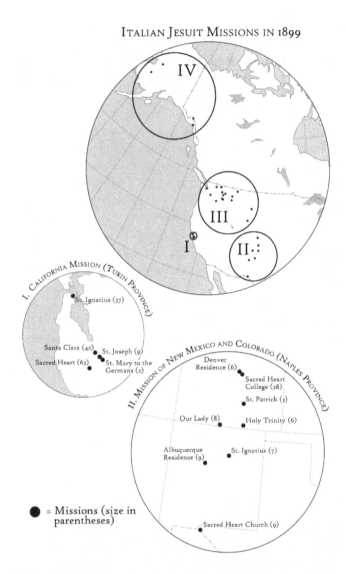

ITALIAN JESUIT MISSIONS IN 1899

IV

III

I

II

I. CALIFORNIA MISSION (TURIN PROVINCE)

St. Ignatius (37)

Santa Clara (42)   St. Joseph (9)
Sacred Heart (63)   St. Mary to the
Germans (2)

II. MISSION OF NEW MEXICO AND COLORADO (NAPLES PROVINCE)

Denver
Residence (6)
Sacred Heart
College (28)
St. Patrick (3)

Our Lady (8)   Holy Trinity (6)

Albuquerque
Residence (9)   St. Ignatius (7)

Sacred Heart Church (9)

● = Missions (size in
parentheses)

FIGURE 3.4   Map of the distribution of Italian Jesuits in the United States in 1899. Two Italian provinces—Naples and Turin—operated four mission regions in the United States at the end of the nineteenth century. The Neapolitans, a province of 323 members, maintained a mission in the US Southwest, which in 1899 comprised 76 men in Colorado, New

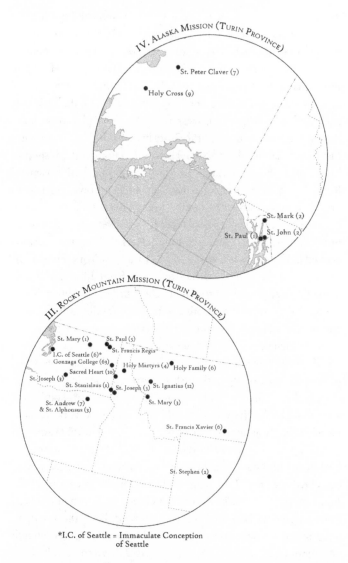

IV. ALASKA MISSION (TURIN PROVINCE)

St. Peter Claver (7)

Holy Cross (9)

St. Mark (2)

St. Paul (1) St. John (2)

III. ROCKY MOUNTAIN MISSION (TURIN PROVINCE)

St. Mary (1)   St. Paul (5)
I.C. of Seattle (6)*   St. Francis Regis
Gonzaga College (63)
Sacred Heart (10)   Holy Martyrs (4) Holy Family (6)
St. Joseph (3)
St. Stanislaus (1) St. Joseph (3) St. Ignatius (12)
St. Andrew (7)   St. Mary (3)
& St. Alphonsus (3)

St. Francis Xavier (6)

St. Stephen (2)

*I.C. of Seattle = Immaculate Conception
of Seattle

Mexico, and Texas. In the same year, the Province of Turin was dispersed across Europe and the United States. Of its 553 members, 153 were in its California mission; 143, in its Rocky Mountain mission; and 21, in its Alaska mission. Source: Map of Italian Jesuit Missions in the United States in 1899, by Geoffrey Wallace, for this volume.

diocese, invited the French Jesuits to take responsibility for Saint Mary's College in Lebanon, Kentucky, in 1831. Flaget's coadjutor, who by the early 1840s was the diocese's leading administrator, Guy Ignatius Chabrat, became increasingly interfering in Jesuit planning. He insisted that the Jesuits open a new school in Louisville, too, a more booming city and where the bishopric itself had moved in 1839. Despite the strain it placed on manpower, the French initiated the short-lived Saint Ignatius Literary Institute in Louisville in 1841. Then John Hughes, the bishop of New York, whose entreaties for Maryland Jesuits Father General Roothaan had been rejected for lack of manpower, turned to French Jesuits, who were looking to invigorate their presence in North America. Clement Boulanger (1790–1868), who as French provincial (1842–45) had sent nine Jesuits to Montreal already, arrived in Kentucky as a visitor in 1845 via New York. Hughes offered to sell the college he had founded, Saint John's, and ultimately Boulanger agreed to buy. In short order, Boulanger closed the Kentucky mission altogether, sent those Jesuits to New York, and then, his task as visitor completed, became the joint superior of the French province's Canada and New York missions.

The Bronx, where Saint John's College was located, was a part of Westchester County until the last quarter of the nineteenth century; and Boulanger quickly realized how important establishing a foothold in the city proper would be to the New York mission. He accordingly assigned the English-born John Larkin (1801–58) to finding a suitable site to the south. With Hughes's approval, Larkin quickly acquired a former Protestant church in Manhattan, dedicated it to the Holy Name of Jesus (echoing the name of the Jesuit mother church in Rome, the Gesù), and opened a school in its basement. Two fires and two churches later, the Jesuits finally found a new location that would last, opening new church and school buildings on West 15th Street in 1850. At Hughes's insistence—"You have your Gesù in Rome outshining Saint Peter's. It must not be so here"—the Jesuits renamed the complex Saint Francis Xavier. It became the hub of Jesuit activity in New York City for the remainder of the century.

When in 1869 the Canada and New York missions became independent of the French province, Johannes Bapst (1815–87) became the superior of what was reconfigured as a combined New York–Canada mission. Bapst's own story is worth a brief diversion. Already ordained, he arrived in the United States in 1848 by a circuitous route from Fribourg in Switzerland. The Maryland provincial who welcomed him was Ignatius Brocard (1793–1852), himself a Swiss refugee, Bapst's former rector in Fribourg, and a former provincial superior of the Upper German province. Brocard assigned Bapst to Maine, where he worked at a mission to the Penobscot people at Old Town as well as with Irish and Canadian Catholics scattered across the state. Bapst attracted the sustained hostility of radical Protestant activists, who targeted him "as a perverter of the young." By opposing the use of Protestant prayers and the King James Version of the Bible in the local public school, they argued, he was "reducing free-born Americans to Rome's galling yoke." The activists, the so-called Know-Nothings, several times attacked Bapst's church and the alternative grammar school for Catholic children that he had founded. In October 1854 they waylaid him on a sick call outside Bangor in Maine, where they tarred and feathered him. A later account explained, "they would most likely have burned him to death had not their supply of matches given out before they could set fire to the brush" tied to him as kindling. A disagreement over Jesuit operations in Maine with the first bishop of Portland led a new Maryland provincial—Burchard Villiger (1819–1903), another Swiss refugee, who had arrived in the United States with Bapst—to withdraw all Jesuits from the state in late 1859. Bapst left to become superior of a newly founded house of studies for Jesuits in Boston and then served as the first president of Boston College between 1863 and 1869.

The new independent mission grew, but as it grew it grew apart. Tensions among the national groups that staffed the mission, a tug-of-war for attention between Montreal and New York City, and an array of difficulties in operating across an international border led to the dissolution of the New York–Canada mission after ten years of existence. At that time, the mission's men were divided between 207 in New York and New Jersey, 130 in Canada and an Indian mission in Sault Ste. Marie, and 60 abroad, mainly in studies in France and Belgium. Bapst's successor as mission superior, Théophile Charaux (1830–1902), returned from New York to Montreal, where he continued as superior of the new Canada mission of the English province. That mission became its own province in 1907. The works and men in the New York part of the mission joined those of the Maryland province. The Maryland provincial, Robert W. Brady (1825–91), moved from Loyola College in Baltimore to Xavier College in Manhattan, where he served out the remainder of his six-year term. The new province—for a year called the New York Province and thereafter the Maryland–New York Province—comprised 526 men stationed from Virginia to Massachusetts. Its largest communities were the houses of formation in Woodstock (130 Jesuits), Frederick (84), and West Park, New York (73). The other largest houses were colleges: Xavier (51), Saint John's (47), and Georgetown (35).

Other French Jesuits, these from the Province of Lyon, arrived in Louisiana in 1836 and a year later opened a college in Grand Coteau (today lying outside Lafayette) for the region's Francophone population. These same Jesuits took over Spring Hill College outside of Mobile, Alabama, in 1846, which the local bishop had founded in 1830. The mission, still staffed with many French priests, was assigned to the Missouri mission in 1838, was reassigned to Lyon province in 1847, was made an independent mission in 1880, and became its own province (New Orleans) in 1907.

German Jesuits

The German Jesuit mission in the United States was distinctive from the others by being least worried about working within a clearly defined geographical area. Although the German missionaries were concentrated along the US banks of the Great Lakes, the mission stations, rather than being contained within a designated region, stretched across the United States from New York to South Dakota. This piggybacking across the mission territories of other provinces was not a new strategy. In the seventeenth and eighteenth centuries, Germany (or, more properly, the Holy Roman Empire and its principalities) was itself not a colonial power. The Jesuit superior general was free to assign missionaries from one country to the colonies of another, and the Spanish Crown was prepared to accept German missionaries. The percentage of German missionaries in the Spanish colonies eventually became so high that the Spanish Crown capped them at 40 percent in 1734, and many German missionaries "Hispanicized" their surnames—for example, Steinhauser to de Pedrosa—to avoid attracting the unwanted attention of colonial bureaucrats. The most famous example of a Jesuit from the Holy Roman Empire serving in New Spain is Eusebio Kino (1645–1711). Kino founded the mission in Pimería Alta, which straddles the modern-day frontier between Arizona and Mexico. Kino was born near Trent, a prince-bishopric within the Holy Roman Empire. Kino's German surname was Kühn, which he Italianized to Chini and then Hispanized to Kino. His education was also in the German-speaking world: he attended school in Innsbruck and was trained as a Jesuit in Freiburg, Ingolstadt, and Landsberg. His missionary work in New Spain began in Baja California and extended to the Pimería Alta, where he died. He made thirty-five expeditions through the Pimería and reported administering about 4,500 baptisms. He introduced new techniques of farming and ranching into the region, and his maps were among the first European maps of the region. On them, he demonstrated to the colonists for the first time that Baja California is a peninsula, not an island (see figure 1 in the preface for an example of the older geographical understanding).

The next wave of German Jesuits arrived in response to the complicated unrest across Europe in the late 1840s, the same unrest that also brought Belgians and Italians to the United States. These Jesuits arrived not as whole provinces but as inspired individuals; and it should be noted that many of them were Swiss.

Often, they arrived to work with the German-speaking immigrant population. A luminary figure in this generation was Burchard Villiger, who was born in the German-speaking Swiss canton of Aargau. Villiger had escaped from Swiss Fribourg after the city capitulated to anticlerical, federalist forces in November 1847; and then again from Turin, after nationalist uprisings there. Many Swiss refugees headed to the United States. Villiger arrived on a ship in New York in June 1848 with others, among whom was the future superior general, Anton Marie Anderledy (1819–92), at the time a deacon. One group, including Anderledy, was sent to Saint Louis. Villiger, in another group, was sent to Washington. Still others settled in the New Orleans mission. Anderledy returned to Europe after two years; but Villiger remained, becoming a leading figure first in the Maryland province, then in the California mission. In the former, he was the president of multiple schools, including the theology school at Woodstock, became a beloved pastor in Philadelphia, and served a term as provincial. He was also sent west to the college at Santa Clara to serve as its president during a period of financial strain and stayed on for several more years as mission superior. He belonged to a class of Catholic clerics in the era that saw the future of the Church in its institutions and was extremely effective at founding and expanding them, literally brick by brick.

Another entry point for Germans into the United States was through the French New York mission, which began staffing churches for German-speaking residents in New York State in 1848. In Buffalo the Jesuits not only provided the local bishop with much needed German-speaking personnel but also helped resolve tensions of long standing between the bishop and several parishes. The dispute was over ownership, and thus operating control, of the parishes, some of which bishops had kept under interdict for years over parishioners' refusal to accede to what they regarded as episcopal interference in their churches. The Jesuits took the bishop's side in the dispute but worked with a tact and artfulness that attenuated resentments on all sides. The

Germans founded Canisius College (subsequently divided into a high school and a college) in Buffalo in 1870, and a year later were constituted into a formal mission of the German province.

The Germans' organization of a formal mission in the United States was encouraged not only by the growing immigrant population but also by new anticlerical hostilities at home. In the mid–nineteenth century, the Catholic Church across Germany was under pressure from formidable, state-sponsored programs of secularization that took their most aggressive form in Otto von Bismarck's Kulturkampf (1871–78). The outcome was far short of Bismarck's own goal to eradicate Catholic influence from politics and culture in the new German Reich. But the so-called Jesuit Law of 1872 seriously restricted the activity of the Jesuits (and other major Catholic orders) there and remained in force until World War I. The anticlerical legislation can, in a certain sense, be credited with creating Jesuits like Eugene Buechel (1874–1954). Buechel left the diocesan seminary in Fulda to enter the German novitiate in exile in the Netherlands in 1897. He was caught up in the exciting prospects of working in the United States; and Jesuit superiors ultimately sent him there, where he studied philosophy in Wisconsin, worked on Indian missions in South Dakota, and studied theology in Saint Louis. After ordination he returned to the Dakotas, where he spent the rest of his life. He was an itinerant preacher, superintended schools, and ran parishes. He also composed dictionaries and grammars of the Indigenous language, collaborated with the famed Catholic medicine man Black Elk, and maintained an extensive correspondence about Lakota culture with the anthropologist Franz Boas. His writings in and about the Lakota language are a precious repository of it; and the thousands of photographs he took record aspects of Lakota culture that all but disappeared in the years following World War II.

The two Indian missions, still in operation today, that captured the imagination and inspired the efforts of so many German Jesuits were the Saint Francis Mission on the Rosebud Reservation and the Holy Rosary Mission (now the Red Cloud Indian

FIGURE 3.5   Eugene Buechel delivers a talk to the delegates of the Owancaya Ominiciye (General Meeting) of the Saints Joseph and Mary's Societies, at the Saint Agnes Mission Church on the Pine Ridge Indian Reservation, 1947. Source: Eugene Buechel at Saint Agnes Mission church, Pine Ridge Indian Reservation, South Dakota, 1947, Marquette University Archives, Milwaukee, Bureau of Catholic Indian Missions Records, ID 10039.

School) on the Pine Ridge Reservation. In both instances the vicar apostolic of Dakota, the Swiss-born Benedictine Martin Marty, was recruiting whatever religious and clergy he could to build up the Church in his isolated territory. The Lakota chiefs—Chief Spotted Tail and his successor, Chief Two Strike, in 1886 at Rosebud, and Chief Red Cloud in 1888 at Pine Ridge—turned to the Jesuits foremost in the hope that they would establish Western-style schools that would prepare a new generation of Native Americans to better negotiate any self-governance and cultural autonomy with the US government. By 1900 the entire German mission in North America comprised, in addition to the two missions in South Dakota (29 Jesuits), a college and parish in Buffalo (57), a college (now Saint Ignatius High School and John Carroll University) and a house of formation in Cleveland (74), a college in Toledo (now Saint John's Jesuit High School) (19), a parish in southern Minnesota (11), and a college and house of studies in Prairie du Chien, Wisconsin (originally, the College of the Sacred Heart; later, Campion Jesuit High School; it closed in 1975) (63).

Before concluding this chapter, a word must be said about that singularly important crisis in nineteenth-century US history, the Civil War. War, of whatever sort, is chaotic, violent, and destructive; and the most basic protection of persons and property becomes a desperate challenge. In this respect, the war affected the Jesuits like many Americans. The Jesuit leadership at the time expressed concern about the disruption the war had on the growth of schools and missions. Several Jesuits served as military chaplains. The New Orleans mission provided four chaplains to the Confederate forces. Darius Hubert (1823–93), a Jesuit from Toulouse who had arrived in New Orleans in 1850, offered public prayers at the Louisiana Secession Convention in 1861 and at the funeral of Jefferson Davis in 1893. During the war he served in Robert E. Lee's Army of Northern Virginia. Six priests from the New York mission and Maryland province joined the Union's military chaplaincy, all but one serving in the field with New York infantry units and the sixth engaging in hospital work in the District of Columbia. A seventh came and went with an abruptness that reveals more about the haphazardness of Jesuit mobility than anything about the order's stance on the war: Jacob Brühl (1811–65), an Austrian, arrived at Saint Charles College in Grand Couteau, Louisiana, in 1856 after eight years at a mission station in Algeria. After serving about twelve months in military hospitals in Union-controlled Beaufort, North Carolina, and New Orleans in 1862 and 1863, he returned to his home province and died within a year at the novitiate in Trnava (now in Slovakia).

Beyond that, there is not much to be said about Jesuits in the Civil War, and the silence speaks volumes. In point of fact, the Jesuits as a group did not declare themselves for one side or the other. No explanation for that neutrality is self-evident. The hard part is actually figuring out why the Jesuits did not do the obvious . . . and officially favor the Confederacy. After all, the order,

JESUITS IN EASTERN AND CENTRAL NORTH AMERICA, 1899

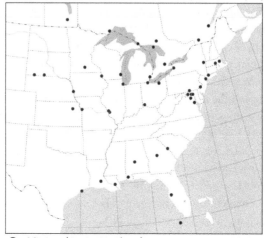

● = Missions (size in parentheses)

MISSOURI PROVINCE

Milwaukee (27)   Detroit (26)

Chicago (54)

Omaha (17)

Cincinnati (38)

St. Mary's (39)

Florissant (147)

Kansas City (4)   St. Louis (173)

* Missions not affiliated with the Missouri Province indicated with gray points

GERMAN MISSION IN NORTH AMERICA

Mankate (11)   Buffalo (45/12)

St. Francis (14)

Holy Rosary (15)   Prairie du   Toledo (19)   Cleveland (34)
Chien (63)

South Brooklyn (40)

* Missions not affiliated with the GMNA indicated with gray points

FIGURE 3.6   Map of Jesuits in the Eastern and Central United States, 1899. In addition to the Italians, the German province was the other European one assigning significant manpower to the United States. In 1899, the German province numbered 1,400 men, none of whom could be missioned to work at home; 244 of them composed its North America

CANADA MISSION

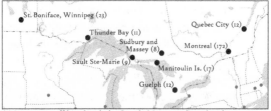

St. Boniface, Winnipeg (23)

Thunder Bay (11)

Quebec City (12)

Sudbury and Massey (8)

Montreal (172)

Sault Ste-Marie (9)

Manitoulin Is. (17)

Guelph (12)

* Missions not affiliated with the Canada Mission indicated with gray points

MARYLAND-NEW YORK PROVINCE

Troy (8)

Boston (46)

Worcester (43)

Keyser Island (5)

New York (118)

Jersey City (20)

Frederick (111)

Philadelphia (35)

Conewago (3)

Woodstock (150)

Baltimore (24)

Washington (71)

Leonardtown (9)

NEW ORLEANS MISSION

Augusta (4)

Macon (32)

Selma (4)

Mobile (36)

Grand Coteau (50)

New Orleans (39)

Galveston (19)

Tampa (13)

Key West (2)

© G. Wallace Cartography & GIS
Map by Geoffrey Wallace, 2022

mission. The rest of upper North America was covered by the Maryland–New York province (634 Jesuits), the Missouri province (487), and the independent missions of New Orleans (223) and Canada (273). Source: Map of Jesuits in the eastern and central United States in 1899, by Geoffrey Wallace, for this volume.

it will be recalled from the previous chapter, was a significant slaveholding entity in the early nineteenth century and continued holding people in bondage across the South until the end of the war. It is true that the order's membership (approaching 800 in the United States at the outbreak of the war) and institutional commitments were geographically diversifying: Jesuits were successfully recruiting from across the United States, and the high percentage of foreign-born Jesuits softened regional attachments to one side or the other of the debates that led to war. Institutions straddled the line separating freedom and slavery from coast to coast. Still, the order's gravitational center was in the South: its only two universities and two of its three novitiates, for example, were in areas with legal slavery. Moreover, distaste for the abolitionists was common among Jesuits and knew no geographical distinction. The antipathy was in large part a reaction to the anti-Catholicism of the abolitionists, who in polemically Protestant terms regarded Catholicism itself as a form of spiritual enslavement. A distressing irony on this point is that many enslaved Black families were Catholic, and many such families had initially been baptized into the faith by earlier generations of Jesuits who owned them or ministered to their owners. In the final analysis, neutrality toward the war and its causes might best be interpreted as a strategy to keep the Jesuits from falling into a civil war of their own: with limited success, local superiors, and even reportedly the superior general, forbad Jesuits from discussing the war in communities. In addition to keeping peace in communities, the silence avoided stirring up the hostile attention of their white neighbors on either side. A preceding century's worth of experience in Europe seemingly offered them a lesson: the effects of contradicting local sentiment on matters of great moment could be deadly. Nonetheless, Jesuit neutrality did not avoid critical attention. The era's most prominent Catholic convert and the one Catholic abolitionist of note, Orestes Brownson, denounced Jesuit silence on the war and its causes as cowardice in 1864. How, he wondered over the course of several lengthy essays, could the Jesuits quietly watch "the nation rent asunder and destroyed by a rebellion which every principle of our religion . . . condemns"?

The Jesuit history of the nineteenth century in the United States was one of great expansion. The possibilities for life and work were wide-ranging; Jesuits recognized and engaged them. Their accomplishment in growing the Church across the United States was prodigious. It was due to talent, creativity, energy, and enormous doses of good fortune. It was also due to productive, if sometimes complicated, relations with US bishops. Their support and endorsement of Jesuit expansion were essential to the order's nineteenth-century successes. Finally, it was due to misfortune abroad. Europe's internecine conflicts over politics and religion—in Belgium, in Italy, in France, and in Germany—worked to America's great benefit, no less within society in general than within the Church and Society of Jesus. By the end of the nineteenth century, however, a demographic change was under way: the flow of refugee personnel was waning but was being made up and surpassed through homegrown recruits. Just as the Church was becoming more American, so, too, were the Jesuits in America. But how would this influence their works, their relationship with the universal Society, and their relationship with larger American society? These continued as the pressing questions of the next century.

FURTHER READING

Primary Literature

Lakotas, Black Robes, and Holy Women: German Reports from the Indian Missions in South Dakota, 1886–1900. Ed. Karl Markus Kreis. Trans. Corinna Dally-Starna. Introduction by Raymond A. Bucko. Omaha: University of Nebraska Press, 2007. This volume collects and translates a cross-section of documents produced by the earliest generation of Jesuits and Franciscans (the Sisters of Saint Francis of Penance and Christian Charity) on the Pine Ridge and Rosebud reservations in the Dakotas.

Life, Letters and Travels of Father Pierre-Jean de Smet, SJ, 1801–1873. Ed. Hiram Martin Chittenden and Alfred Talbot Richardson. 3 vols. New York: Harper, 1905. Also available online and as a reprint.

Secondary Literature

Garraghan, Gilbert J. *The Jesuits of the Middle United States*. 3 vols. New York: America Press, 1938. A three-volume work that presents the spread of Jesuit activities across the Mississippi River watershed in the nineteenth century. Garragahn is most thorough on the Missouri mission/province but also details the Italian missions of the Northwest and the California coast, as well as the French missions from Kentucky to the Gulf Coast.

Jeffrey, Katherine Bentley. *First Chaplain of the Confederacy: Father Darius Hubert, SJ*. Baton Rouge: Louisiana State University Press, 2020. This study adds to the growing research into Catholic attitudes toward the Civil War and its causes.

Killoren, John J. *"Come, Blackrobe": De Smet and the Indian Tragedy*. Norman: University of Oklahoma Press, 1994. Killoren's *"Come, Blackrobe"* tells the story of "the Indian tragedy" almost exclusively from De Smet's missionary perspective. De Smet is a figure who warrants the considerable attention that is paid to him, and Killoren's historical analysis is substantive and critical.

Markowitz, Harvey. *Converting the Rosebud: Catholic Mission and the Lakotas, 1886–1916*. Civilization of the American Indian Series, Volume 277. Norman: University of Oklahoma Press, 2018. Markowitz tells the story of the Saint Francis Mission on the Rosebud Reservation in front of the background of national-level conflicts between the Catholic Church and the Protestant organizations over appropriate strategies of conversion and assimilation.

McKevitt, Gerald. *Brokers of Culture: Italian Jesuits in the American West, 1848–1919*. Stanford, CA: Stanford University Press, 2007. McKevitt's work covers both European and North American sides of the history of the many Italian Jesuits who came to the United States and Indian Territories in the nineteenth century. The migrations of other Jesuit ethnic groups enjoy no comparable work. Given the primary interest of the Italian Jesuits in missions to the Indigenous peoples, the middle chapters of this work are important for drawing attention to an underappreciated and complex dimension of nineteenth-century Jesuit history in upper North America. It serves also as an excellent history of the development of a Jesuit presence on the West Coast.

Peterson, Jacqueline. *Sacred Encounters: Father De Smet and the Indians of the Rocky Mountain West.* Norman: University of Oklahoma Press, 1993. This volume comprises a beautiful collection of photographs of materials—maps and other documents, images of persons and places, and artifacts—held mainly at the Jesuit Archives and Research Center in Saint Louis.

Steltenkamp, Michael F. *Nicholas Black Elk: Medicine Man, Missionary, Mystic.* Norman: University of Oklahoma Press, 2009. Black Elk was an Oglala Lakota who survived the Battle of Little Big Horn in 1876 and was wounded at the massacre at Wounded Knee in 1890. He claimed extensive religious visions from a young age. He embraced Catholicism in 1904. As a lay catechist, he evangelized and baptized hundreds of his fellow Lakota. Steltenkamp (1947–), himself a Jesuit priest who worked many years on the Pine Ridge Reservation, where Black Elk spent much of his adult life, offers a spiritual biography of the famed holy man. He presents him as a striking synthesis of Native and Christian spiritual insight and expression.

4

Upswing, 1900–1960

———

THE EARLY TWENTIETH CENTURY marks a coming of age both for the US Church and the US Jesuits. Two analogous decisions in Rome signal this development. The Holy See made the first, when in 1908 it removed US dioceses from the oversight of the office for mission territories, the Sacred Congregation for the Propagation of the Faith. This decision acknowledged the growing Catholic population and network of Catholic institutions in the United States. It was also a sign of Vatican confidence in the US bishops. The second was a decision internal to the Society and implemented in 1915 to organize the US provinces into their own "assistancy." An assistancy is a grouping of provinces that work together on common projects and that the superior general handles as a unit in many matters. Its erection marked the culmination of nearly a decade of administrative reconfigurations that reduced the formal connections of provinces and missions in the United States to European provinces. The creation of the American Assistancy was a recognition in Rome that a set of aspirations, challenges, and resources united US Jesuits and required their coordinated management.

While both decisions were highly administrative, neither was merely administrative. Both were related to the question of how the minority Church should grow and assimilate into the great American melting pot. At the end of the nineteenth century the Holy See had condemned a version of assimilation known as "Americanism," which seemed to endorse uncritically an American model of individual liberties and the separation of church and state. The Jesuit theologians at Woodstock, it will be recalled from the previous chapter, supported Rome's condemnation; but there were scarcely any other indications of Catholic isolation in such Jesuit works as schools and missions that brought the order into ordinary contact with non-Catholics. What required development, however, was a more robust strategy to help Catholics fully participate in, benefit from, and even shape American civic and economic life. Catholics had of course been doing that since Lord Baltimore's negotiations over religious liberty in his colony three centuries earlier; in the twentieth century, new circumstances, both inside and outside the Church, created new challenges and new possibilities. New strategies entailed careful navigation between the often-incompatible expectations of Roman authorities, the dominant American Protestant elite, and the diverse American Catholic population itself.

PROVINCES AND JESUIT TRAINING

The combination of Jesuit migration to the United States and home-grown recruits led to significant growth in membership at the turn of the century. The number of Jesuits in the United States—twenty-six hundred at the century's outset—had tripled since the Civil War. Largely unchanged since the war, two domestic provinces, one independent mission, and five missions dependent on three European provinces organized these Jesuits' life and work. By 1920, the governing structure, organized as the new American Assistancy, had been consolidated to four provinces. These four provinces encompassed the entire continental United States and Alaska, but an even distribution of manpower was neither a goal nor the reality. New York City's gravitational pull shaped the Maryland–New York province, even with men distributed among many cities on the East Coast: the provincial resided at Xavier College in Manhattan, and the novitiate had relocated in 1903 from Frederick, Maryland, to Poughkeepsie, New York. Burgeoning novitiate entrances necessitated a short-lived novitiate at Yonkers, New York, which was replaced with a novitiate near Lenox, Massachusetts, opened in 1923, and another in Wernersville, Pennsylvania, opened in 1930. Jesuits selected these latter locations, at some remove from New York City, in anticipation of the thriving province's future division into three. The theologate at Woodstock (227 Jesuits) followed Poughkeepsie (281) in size. The largest five apostolic communities were at the colleges—Boston, Fordham, Georgetown, Holy Cross, and Xavier—each of which had about twenty-five priests. The province had in part grown by taking over the eastern half of the German mission, including Canisius College in Buffalo, in 1907. By 1920 it also operated a mission of its own in Jamaica. The central and western portions of the German mission fell to the Missouri province, as did parts of the Neapolitan mission in the American Southwest. The men and works in Cleveland, Denver, and the Dakota missions were thus added to the country's second-oldest province. Missouri's provincial resided in Saint Louis; the province's major houses of formation were Saint Louis University (255 Jesuits, with the university) and Saint Stanislaus (170) in Florissant, and its five largest apostolic houses were at the schools in Saint Louis; Chicago (53); Prairie du Chien, Wisconsin (43); Saint Mary's, Kansas (42); and Milwaukee (41).

Two additional provinces emerged in this period out of the European missions. Constituted out of the three missions of the Turin province in 1915, the new California province ran along the Pacific Coast from Los Angeles north and included extensive missions in Alaska. Its provincial resided in Portland, its novitiate was outside Santa Clara, its largest single residence was a house of studies in Spokane (151 Jesuits), and its largest communities connected to works were the colleges in San Francisco (33), Santa Clara (33), and Spokane (41). The New Orleans province had its own rich tradition as a mission, sometimes domestic and sometimes French. It took over some responsibilities from the suppressed Neapolitan mission in the US Southwest, maintaining residences in Albuquerque and El Paso and briefly operating a seminary and college for the local bishop in Galveston. Its provincial resided in New Orleans; its novitiate was in Macon, Georgia; and it sent its scholastics mainly to Spokane, Saint Louis, and Woodstock for their studies. Other than houses of formation and New Orleans itself, which was home to 51 Jesuits at Immaculate Conception College (now Jesuit High School) and Loyola College (founded in 1904, now Loyola University), the four largest concentrations of Jesuits were at the colleges in Mobile, Alabama (Spring Hill, 37 Jesuits); Tampa (16); Grand Coteau, Louisiana (33); and the residences in El Paso (21), where from 1915 to 1942 the Jesuit Anthony Joseph Schuler (1869–1944) served as the diocese's founding bishop.

By mid-century, the number of provinces had increased to ten, and their geographic distribution gives an indication of what was still more faintly emerging in the nineteenth century and was quite unsettled before that, namely, how the growth and concerns of the domestic Catholic population were driving Jesuits' own growth and concerns: On the East Coast, there were now three provinces: the New England province, centered in Boston, was established in 1926; and what remained was divided into the New York and Maryland provinces in 1943. The Maryland provincialate returned to Baltimore, and Washington became home to the largest contingent of Jesuits in that province. Out of the Missouri province, the Chicago province was founded in 1928, and out of it the Detroit province was formed in 1956. The Wisconsin province was formed out of Missouri, in 1955. The California province split into the California and Oregon provinces in 1932. The number of men and institutions in the California province led to speculation, never realized, that it could be divided into Los Angeles and San Francisco provinces. For nine years (1960–69), a Buffalo province existed as an eleventh province, a legacy of the old German mission.

To the house of studies at Woodstock were added three more: in the town of Weston outside Boston in 1922; in Alma near Santa Clara in 1934; and in West Baden Springs, Indiana, some 50 miles outside Louisville in 1934. All these were founded in the country-side, following not as much the proclivity of an earlier generation for the countryside but a notion held more broadly in the Church that the training of priests ought to be at some remove from the seeming decadence and distractions of the city. That mood, burgeoning enrollment, and the attendant need for economically acquirable property encouraged the Missouri province to move its theologate in 1931 from the city of Saint Louis to the small town of Saint Mary's in Kansas, where the Jesuits had, almost a century before, founded a mission to the Potawatomi. That the archbishop of Chicago also invited the Jesuits to take on instruc-tional responsibilities at his seminary at Mundelein, Illinois, gives evidence of the abundance of men available for instruction and the confidence of the American hierarchy in the Society's work.

With 7,754 Jesuits in the United States, the order was close to its demographic high point in 1955, nationally as well as globally. Not only were the Jesuits at their largest numbers objectively, sig-nificant proportions were likewise peaking at mid-century in the United States: there were three scholastics to every four priests, one US priest in twelve was a Jesuit, and there was one Jesuit to every nine thousand faithful. The surge in home-grown vocations in the early twentieth century awaits a scholarly explanation, not only in the Society but across Western seminaries and congrega-tions, male and female. It bears noting that these generations of postwar priestly vocation also diminished significantly in size in the late 1960s and 1970s through departures from the priesthood and separation from religious congregations. A half century later, they became most closely associated with the scandals of clerical misconduct and its mishandling by bishops and superiors. In the meantime, the expansion of institutional commitments on the basis of the rising numbers of Jesuits was prodigious. These new commitments indicate that the boom's ultimate transience and its abrupt end were not anticipated. Already in the late 1950s, the surge in vocations was receding in parts of Western Europe. In the United States, the drop took another decade to hit, and it hit hard. But we are running ahead of our story. For the moment, the growth in personnel fueled the expansion of Jesuit commitments to both old and new works, aspects of which we will now turn.

THE MISSIONS

In the early twentieth century, the Jesuit provinces in the United States changed from being principally the recipient of missionary Jesuits to being their donor to other parts of the world. This transition corresponded to the pope's declaration that the United States was no longer mission territory as well as to new ecclesiastical energy being invested in the missions globally. In the 1910s and 1920s, fresh thought was given across the Church to the goals and methods of missionary work: academic chairs in the new theological subfield of missiology were created in the Catholic theology department at Münster in 1910, at the school in Rome operated by the papal office responsible for Catholic mission territories in 1920, and at the Jesuits' own Gregorian University in 1929. With such developments in the background, the superior general, Wlodimir Ledóchowski (1866–1942, r. 1914–42), turned in 1916 to the United States to encourage American Jesuits to consider volunteering for missions beyond their national borders.

The idea of US Jesuits in missions was not entirely new. Jesuits had been active in the Indian territories and the reservation system throughout the nineteenth century. Such work was considered "missionary." The Italian Jesuits expanded this mission into the Alaska territory in 1886. Then, Jamaica's assignment to the Maryland–New York province in 1893 marks the first foreign mission to fall to the care of the US provinces. The Missouri province took responsibility for British Honduras in 1894, and then Patna, India, in 1921. Since the superior general in Rome directed the allotment of Jesuit missions, the shifting assignment of territories can appear like an ecclesiastical version of the boardgame Risk. Shortly after the Bombay mission was assigned to Maryland–New York, it became clear that access for missionaries of US citizenship would be difficult to obtain. To solve that problem, the superior general reassigned the Americans to the Philippines, thus freeing the Jesuits of the Aragon province who had been working there to go to Bombay. The Philippines, moreover, was soon to become a refuge for missionaries exiled from China, including a large group of Maryknoll Fathers, after their expulsion early in the Chinese Civil War (1927–37). The newly established Communist Party regime expelled the Jesuits again in 1949, including Californians who had been there since 1928. The New England province established a mission in Baghdad, which

FIGURE 4.1 Wilfrid Le Sage with refugees outside Nanjing, 1949. In the final stage of the Chinese Civil War, with Nationalist forces in retreat, the People's Liberation Army (Communist) crossed the Yangtze River and entered the Nationalist capital Nanjing without opposition on April 23, 1949. Here, the California Jesuit Wilfrid Le Sage (1907–80) stands with refugees outside the city before its fall. An estimated 40,000 refugees were living in camps outside the city. Le Sage obtained a weapons carrier and transformed it into an ambulance and ministered to them. Throughout early 1949, the Jesuits moved scholastics to safe locations outside China, mainly to the Philippines. Source: Wilfrid Le Sage with refugees outside Nanjing, 1949, JARC, California Province Archives, China Mission Collection, 1320-34-28-001b.

FIGURE 4.2   Lloyd Lorio at the Eastern Technical Institute in Sri
Lanka, 1972. The French province of Champagne founded the mission
of Trincomalee-Batticaloa (Ceylon, now Sri Lanka) in 1893. The New
Orleans province took over the mission in 1946. The mission became
freestanding as a vice province in 1962 and exists today as the province of
Sri Lanka. At mid-century, the mission included a college, a retreat house,
and ten rural mission stations. Lorio (1927–2021) arrived in 1951. He
helped found the Eastern Technical Institute in Batticaloa, whose students
are featured with a milling machine in this photograph. With the growth
of indigenous vocations, the mission became a vice province. Lorio remained till his death in 2021. Source: Lloyd Lorio at the Eastern Technical
Institute in in Sri Lanka, 1972, JARC, New Orleans Province Archives,
Open File 003.

included two schools, in 1932. Those US Jesuits remained there
until a new Baathist government came to power by coup (which
brought Saddam Hussein to prominence) and expelled them in
1969. Irish Jesuits declined an offer to take over for the expelled
Americans. New Orleans Jesuits headed to Ceylon (Sri Lanka);

Wisconsin Jesuits, to Korea. At mid-century, one in six US Jesuits was working in the foreign missions, and one in seven Jesuits in the missions was from the American Assistancy. The institutional numbers are likewise staggering from our point of view today: The US provinces directed 16 missions, which encompassed 15 institutions of higher learning and advanced technical training, 6 seminaries for local clergy, 66 high schools, 280 elementary schools, 71 medical dispensaries, 198 mission churches, 24 hospitals, and 26 orphanages.

EDUCATION

The early twentieth century was the opening of a booming era for the educational work of the US Jesuits, but matters began on a rough note. The underlying problem was one of "Americanization," and at its heart was the question of how the Jesuits wanted their schools to fit in the US system of education. On the one hand, the Jesuits had a time-tested educational model, founded on the *Ratio studiorum*, which was a set of guidelines for school administrators and a humanistic curriculum that dated from the late sixteenth century. On the other hand, educational developments in the United States and Europe made the *Ratio* seem not just distinctive but also distinctively ill-suited to modern needs and pedagogical trends. Two intertwined crises at the end of the nineteenth century forced the question of reform: first, in 1893 Harvard Law School, in amending its admission procedure, identified 102 schools whose bachelor degrees were considered adequate for admission without further examination. The list originally included no Catholic schools and by the end of the century included only two, Georgetown University and the Holy Cross Fathers' University of Notre Dame in Indiana. Catholic educators were stunned. When the president of Holy Cross College pressed his counterpart at Harvard, the dynamic and blustery Charles William Eliot, for an explanation, he retorted, "Graduates of Boston, Holy Cross, and Fordham would not be admitted even to the Junior Class of Harvard College."

Eliot explained his rejection of the Jesuit curriculum in an essay in *The Atlantic Monthly*. He cited its stultifying religious origins and antiquated lack of commitment to the sciences. Timothy Brosnahan (1865–1915), a philosopher and former president of Boston College, responded in the Catholic press, condemning the new Harvard curriculum as pedagogically lazy for its small set of required courses and capriciously abundant electives. The exchange garnered national attention but fostered no change of the Harvard faculty's mind. Then, at roughly the same time, another slap came from closer to home: an 1898 survey revealed that the majority of Catholics attending college were enrolled in non-Catholic institutions. A startling new explanation was now at hand for many Jesuit colleges' enrollment deficiencies, and an old one had been weakened: it was not that Catholics lacked all encouragement to go to college; it was that they were willing to be educated elsewhere.

These coincident critiques of Jesuit education gave a sense of urgency to a problem that had been brewing for some time. The order had to face a set of serious questions about what effect they wanted their schools to have on their students, how tightly they wanted to hew to the educational program laid out in the *Ratio studiorum*, and whether they wanted their schools on the sidelines or in the mainstream of the burgeoning American educational system. Complicating matters was of course the tribal rivalry lurking in the background between the Protestant elite, embodied by Eliot, and the Catholic immigrants. That rivalry worked hand in hand on the Jesuit psyche with Rome's hostility toward what was regarded as Protestant-inspired modernism.

The approach taken by the Jesuits over the next few decades was genuinely middle of the road. There was resistance and force from all sides, but the ultimate result for Jesuit schools was a look more like their secular American counterparts than before. As it was, a Jesuit general congregation in Rome had in 1906 rejected the call for a revised and universally implemented *Ratio* on the grounds that modern circumstances made such narrow standardization impractical. A study subsequently undertaken at

Woodstock College on the *Ratio studiorum* revealed that there was more variety in its application around the globe than previously assumed anyway. The US schools adjusted their curricula to incorporate more natural sciences and to realign their year-by-year requirements to correspond to mainstream standards. The schools also expanded to include more practical curricula, the forerunners of later business and extension schools. Saint John's College in New York City, for example, pushed hard against local resistance to a business curriculum that its faculty had been developing since the 1880s; and Georgetown expanded both its scientific courses to include more mathematics and sciences and its humanities courses to include more in modern languages. Jesuit governance began encouraging, albeit with limited success, scholastics to pursue higher degrees beyond the disciplines of theology, philosophy, and ancient languages and even to earn them at secular institutions. To accomplish these curricular changes quickly, school administrators began recruiting faculty more than ever from outside the order. The superior general gave the accommodations an approving nod in a letter on education to the US provincials in 1934.

New lay involvement in the running of the schools in this period included not only the intensified hiring of lay faculty but also new consultative structures. Throughout the nineteenth century, schools had been managed through an internal Jesuit structure, within which the local rector with a group of advisers (called consultors) directed operations. Beginning in the twentieth century, schools began to establish consultative bodies of lay Catholics, which provided practical advice for the operation of the schools, helped recruit new students, and aided their better job placement after graduation. Many Jesuit schools began more actively seeking out non-Catholics to augment their predominantly Catholic student bodies.

Another structural change under way early in the century was the separation of high schools from colleges. At the end of the nineteenth century, Jesuit schools offered a seven-year program divided into upper and lower schools, usually located together.

Outside the Catholic orbit and beginning at the end of the nineteenth century, US education was moving toward an eight-year program, divided between two separate four-year institutions. By World War I, Jesuit schools had begun adopting this programmatic division in response to the increasing expectation at mainstream universities that incoming students have a four-year "high school" education behind them. The discussion of dividing Jesuit schools this way opened up a debate over the distribution of manpower and the possibility of concentrating Jesuits more strategically at particular schools. An idea circulated that a number of upper schools should be suppressed, but their corresponding lower schools should be left open to serve as feeder schools for the fewer, stronger upper schools that remained. In New Orleans, for example, the Jesuits made a limited reorganization of their schools at the time: at Immaculate Conception College, founded in 1847, the upper school was suppressed in 1911; and the lower school was preserved as a four-year secondary school (today, Jesuit High School). The newer Loyola College, founded in 1904, was then restructured as a university and incorporated in 1912 as Loyola University. In closing any well-established schools, New Orleans was the exception rather than the rule.

At the beginning of the twentieth century, the US Jesuits claimed 35 colleges under their direction, including ones in Honduras and Jamaica. Half a century later, the Assistancy boasted 30,000 students in 42 high schools and 100,000 students in 27 universities. Several of the universities were new foundations, such as Le Moyne College in Syracuse in 1946. Others had been received from local bishops. In this latter category, Saint Vincent College in Los Angeles was ultimately rechartered, divided, and expanded as Loyola High School and Loyola University; and at the University of Scranton, the Jesuits succeeded the Lasallian Christian Brothers, who withdrew from the school in 1942. The universities included schools of business, adult education, medicine and dentistry, engineering, and even aeronautical technology. The increase in students in the first half of the twentieth century came from the increasing Catholic population, which had grown from 12 million to 29 million. University enrollments dramatically increased after World War II on account of veterans, whose education the GI Bill funded as a federal benefit. A glance outside the larger cities serves also to remind that a number of Jesuit schools flourished for reasons quite independent of all that was at stake in the earlier controversies with Eliot and of the burgeoning Catholic population of European descent: Schools for Native American youths could be found in six western states plus Alaska, and Jesuits had founded academies in New Mexico and California to educate Spanish speakers whose numbers were increasing due to northward migration in the 1910s, in part a result of the Mexican Civil War.

Spiritual Ministries, Popular Religion, and the Catholic Press

Outside the schools, the principal forms of pastoral outreach to lay adult Catholics took two forms in the early twentieth century: the parish mission and the lay retreat. Such pastoral practice had its roots in the colonial practice of Jesuit priests' traveling on a circuit to thinly dispersed Catholic populations whom they catechized and to whom they administered the sacraments. In the nineteenth century, Jesuits tended to particular immigrant groups, most notably Germans, in this way. By the end of the nineteenth century, traveling preachers were taking the form of "mission bands," groups of priests who traveled to congregations that parish priests already served but who wanted the benefit of a structured weekend of sermons and devotions, reminiscent of a Protestant revival.

The first Jesuit to take on such a ministry with a national scope was Arnold Damen. He held his first parish mission at Saint Mary's Cathedral in Chicago in 1857 and, along with two Jesuit companions, began traveling across the country in the first "mission band" to English-speaking Catholics. The program stayed popular through the 1910s, and all the provinces assigned men to this work. The demand was so great, among both laity and clergy, that superiors complained that if they acceded to every request for a mission, they would have no priests left to staff anything else. Interest wavered in the interwar years, revived briefly after World War II, and waned again at mid-century. The Jesuits addressed the decline in the 1960s, at which point New England was the only province to assign priests in numbers to mission bands. The conclusion: the bands had served their purpose. Parishes had other means of spiritual renewal; and the format, it was curiously suggested, was not suited to Jesuits.

The era also saw the beginnings of a robust retreat movement. In the previous century, the retreat ministry was closely associated with parish missions. At the end of that century, there was one retreat house designated as such in the nation, the Manresa Institute on Keyser Island in Connecticut. Opened in 1889, it offered programs of three to five days consisting of liturgies, points for prayer given in lecture form, and time for private prayer. It catered mainly to Jesuits, diocesan clergy, and students from Jesuit schools. Lay men on retreat constituted only the most occasional exception. The buildings and grounds doubled as a summer school and vacation camp for Jesuits in training.

At the turn of the century, Europeans were more actively developing a retreat program for lay people. In early 1909, members of New York's Xavier Alumni sodality approached the Jesuits with a request for a retreat on the model of what the English Jesuits were doing. In response, the provincial appointed Terence J. Shealy (1863–1922)—a Jesuit whose association with another movement, the labor school movement, was not accidental and will be returned to presently—to the task. Shealy held a first day of spiritual conferences for a select group of eighteen men from diverse corners of New York society in July. The talks were inspired by Saint Ignatius's collection of meditations, the Spiritual Exercises, and were applied to issues of contemporary social concern. Shealy touched on themes related to the tension for American Catholics between their religious identity and their participation in a civil society that was in the main hostile to them. Shealy infused his reflections with the popes' developing social teachings and hardening opposition to communism. Shealy's program garnered enthusiasm, and he persuaded his group to organize as the Laymen's League for Retreats and Social Studies. After two years of growing success but peripatetic operation, the league acquired its own facility, on Staten Island and dubbed Mount Manresa, the first retreat house for the laity in the nation, and the beginning of a trend.

The model of Shealy's retreats and retreat houses expanded to an ever-broader Catholic clientele. The content of these retreats drew themes from Catholic moral teaching: sin, forgiveness, the sacraments, virtues, and vices. Retreats were structured around sermons; daily mass and confession were sacramental highlights. The movement's aim of spiritual perfection went hand in hand with what in 1951 the former California provincial Zacheus Maher (1882–1963) called its "consequent" aim, the strengthening of "the social order." That social order, Maher made clear with reference to writings of Pius XI and Pius XII, was under threat from atheism and communism. Retreat houses were to be a bulwark against them. What began as eighteen men meeting with Shealy in the Bronx became by mid-century seventeen retreat houses from coast to coast, which offered over 300 retreats to more than 13,000 retreatants each year. To this can be added per annum about 500 additional retreats that Jesuits were offering to 30,000 retreatants in houses run by dioceses and other congregations.

An expansion of the popular Catholic press also marked the early century. *The Messenger of the Sacred Heart*, a monthly with a devotional bent, had been published since 1865. John J. Wynne (1859–1948) took singlehandedly to expanding this publishing outreach to the general public. He developed a companion magazine of more practical religious interest, called simply *Messenger*, in 1905. His greatest achievement was as founding editor of the *Catholic Encyclopedia*, a scholarly compendium of Catholic doctrine, history, and culture, whose first volume appeared in 1907, and which in revised form is maintained to this day. In the midst of that project, Wynne turned to founding a new weekly, which he and his advisers envisioned as an American version of the British Catholic *Tablet*. The first issue of the news weekly *America* appeared in April 1909. Its editorial slant in the early years was generally progressive in politics and economics, culturally conservative, and tribally protective. It engaged the editors of the *Encyclopedia Britannica* in an extended controversy in the 1910s over the anti-Catholic slant of numerous articles. It bemoaned expansion of the franchise to women in the Nineteenth Amendment to the US Constitution in 1920, concerned that "the grimy 'game' of politics" would "vulgarize and coarsen woman's fine nature." It supported the pro-Church but also fascist nationalist faction in the Spanish Civil War in the 1930s. It endorsed central components of Roosevelt's New Deal, such as the National Industrial Recovery Act, which was aimed at developing codes of fair competition and pricing, and the Bankhead Bill, whose goal was to assist the transformation of tenant farmers and farm laborers into landowners. Its most consequential early editor was arguably Francis X. Talbot (1889–1953), from 1936 to 1944. In addition to guiding the journal through the late New Deal and World War II, Talbot was committed to invigorating its reviews of literature and culture, including of film. Talbot proved himself further influential by initiating the discussions that led to the founding of another Jesuit periodical, the scholarly journal *Theological Studies*, in 1940.

An especially popular form of outreach the Jesuits undertook in this period was the sodality movement. Jesuits had developed the sodality in the sixteenth century as a way of encouraging spiritual fervor among the Catholic laity. Inspired by insights of Saint Ignatius, sodalities fostered among their members frequent examination of conscience, prayer, and reception of the sacraments, as well as a commitment to the spiritual and corporal works of mercy. In the United States, it was organized as the Sodality of the Blessed Virgin Mary. Its headquarters was in Saint Louis. Units of the sodality arose in schools, parishes, and workplaces across the country. Priests, nuns, and school teachers served as moderators of the local units. The Sodality operated its own press, which published

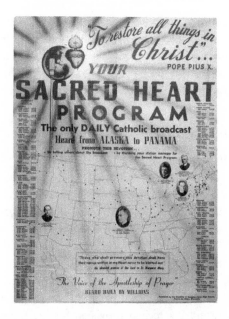

FIGURE 4.3   Advertisement for the Sacred Heart radio program (1940s?). This 15-minute program was a morning prayer service consisting of hymns, a consecration of the day to the Sacred Heart, the Angelus, and a brief sermon. Eugene P. Murphy (1892–1973) began broadcasting the service from the Saint Louis University campus radio station, WEW, in 1939. The Sacred Heart Club Program came to encompass an international network of broadcast stations. Students from Campion High School in Prairie du Chien, Wisconsin, drafted the map in the advertisement. Programming ended in 2005. Source: Advertisement for the Sacred Heart radio program. JARC, Missouri Province Archives, Sacred Heart Program.

a periodical, *The Queen's Work*, and materials for prayer and retreats, as well as commentary on issues of social and moral concern. In 1925 the charismatic and indefatigable Jesuit Daniel A. Lord (1888–1955) was assigned to lead the Sodality. He was inspired by a concern for the spiritual well-being of Catholic youth, the papal call for Catholic engagement in the public sphere, and a profound worry over totalitarian political movements in Christian lands. He wrote hundreds of pamphlets on Catholic doctrine and practice; founded the Summer Schools of Catholic Action,

attracted hundreds of thousands of participants
helped draft the Production Code for motion
laid out the criteria for movie ratings followed
States from 1930 to 1968. At its height under his
direction, the Sodality of Our Lady claimed 2 million members.

The Social Question

The "social question" dominated Jesuit conversation in the years after World War I. The US Jesuits were prompted to action from two sides. First, there was a larger conversation within the American Church. The influential *Catechism of the Social Question* (1921) by John A. Ryan, a diocesan priest and professor at Catholic University in Washington, defined the social question as "evils and grievances affecting the wage-earning classes, and calling for removal or remedy." The grievances included "low wages, long hours, unemployment, industrial autocracy, bad housing, and insufficient provision for the future, . . . the problems of farm tenancy, the drift of population from country to city, the excessive cost of getting food from the producer to the consumer, taxation, divorce, poverty, vocational training—are all social questions." "We cannot make earth heaven," Ryan opined in an indirect critique of communism, "but we can make the life and labor of the masses more humane and more pleasing to God" through "a better distribution: higher wages for the underpaid, social insurance, profit-sharing, copartnership, cooperative production, and taxation . . . [and] insurance against sickness, old age, and unemployment." The Jesuits signed on wholeheartedly.

The other came from the superior general, Ledóchowski, who encouraged the Americans throughout the 1930s to coordinate their forces in the struggle against atheistic communism. In response to a letter from him in April 1934, a group of Jesuits gathered at Loyola University in Chicago. They called for a "united front" against communism through "the establishment of a Christian social order." A few months later, at a similar meeting in West Baden Springs, Indiana, participants advocated an

explicitly confrontational approach by developing a Catholic an-
alogue to the communist "Popular Front." This "United Front"
would "gain control of worthy causes," such as the peace and
labor movements, and use adult education programs as a means
of winning ordinary citizens to their side. Two distinct tacks—
sometimes complementary, sometimes rival—were emerging in
these meetings: one, a more top-down confidence in Christianity's
capacity to solve the social question; the other, imagining a com-
bative mobilization of local communities. Leading advocates
of each strategy were Jesuits, prominent across many fields of
American politics and culture: Edmund Walsh (1885–1956)
and Daniel Lord were advocates of the first strategy. Walsh had
founded Georgetown's School of Foreign Service in 1919, organized papal famine relief to Russia in 1922, mediated for the
pope a resolution to church-state conflicts in Mexico after its civil
war in 1929, and negotiated the opening of a Jesuit high school
in Baghdad in 1931. In later years, he was a confidant of Senator
Joseph McCarthy, who rose to and fell from fame for accusing
various federal agencies of being infiltrated by communists. John
LaFarge (1880–1963), favoring the grassroots strategy, was an
early promoter of civil rights for African Americans. LaFarge will
be returned to shortly.

However dissatisfied the sides might have been with each other,
two observations about the deliberation can to be made. First,
underneath the strategic debates, scores of Jesuits were engaged in
direct outreach exactly along the lines the pope and superior general directed. Taking just one example, Carmelo Tranchese (1880–
1956), a Jesuit from Naples who was trained in Malta and Wales,
arrived in his province's New Mexico–Colorado Mission in 1911,
and he spent the rest of his life in the American Southwest. His most
consequential work was with Hispanic populations in South and
West Texas during the 1930s and 1940s. In those socially tumultuous years, he collaborated with county agencies to ensure that
there were health clinics for the otherwise-neglected populations
of migrant workers, within whose communities tuberculous was
a public health issue of great concern. While generally suspicious

FIGURE 4.4 Carmelo Tranchese with parishioners at a "grocery depot," San Antonio, 1938. Tranchese worked with various Catholic charities to establish such no-cost "grocery depots" in San Antonio in response to massive layoffs by the Southern Pecan Shelling Company in 1938. The layoffs were in retaliation for labor strikes against low wages and poor working conditions earlier in the year and for the new 25 cents-per-hour minimum wage established by the Fair Labor Relations Act in October 1938. Many of the 10,000 laid-off workers were Hispanics who lived in San Antonio's "West Side," where Tranchese was pastor of Our Lady of Guadalupe Church. Source: Carmelo Tranchese with parishioners at a "grocery depot," San Antonio, 1938, JARC, New Orleans Province Archives, A-001.

of labor unions (regarded as Trojan horses for communism), he advocated on behalf of unskilled laborers and supported the pecan workers' strikes of 1935 and 1938. He helped organize the Catholic Relief Association to provide a safety net for families in financial distress. In 1937 he was appointed to the San Antonio Housing Authority, which persuaded the Roosevelt administration to approve a project for the city. When the housing project was completed, Tranchese, who as a scholastic had imagined himself teaching classical languages at a college in his homeland, offered the president an original poem, "the sincere expression of a suffering part of your subjects . . . in return for all you have done to better the conditions of our poor people . . . [in] Latin, the language of the great statesmen and of the heroes." He died of heart failure in Grand Coteau, Louisiana, in 1956.

Second, the rivalry between the two different strategic models appears productive in retrospect. Raymond T. Feely (1895–1965) came to the national discussion with experience working with organized labor in San Francisco. For Feely, the Jesuits required something more than red-baiting, something inspired by a real concern over the exploitation of working people in a time of economic depression and of impoverished social responsibility within business. Taking what he considered the best of both Walsh's and LaFarge's programs, he argued in a report directly to Ledóchowski for a two-front war, and he pointed to European models as a precedent, in a scholarly fashion, like the Belgian Jesuit Arthur Vermeersch's approach in his *Manuel social*, and in a popular way, as exemplified by the Jesuit Gustav Desbuquois's leadership in the *Action populaire*, a center of social action in France. Feely's vision began taking form when the provincials commissioned New Yorker John Delaney (1906–56) to found the Institute of Social Order (ISO) in 1940. The ISO, much as Lédochowski had hoped, was reminiscent of Action populaire in Reims. Among the goals outlined in its founding charter were "to show every Jesuit how in his field social principles could be made a reality" and "to make the whole Society in the United States responsive to the call of the Holy Father . . . and the challenge of our late Father General to take our place in the battle to control the happiness, temporal prosperity, and the eternal safety of the next few generations." At its beginning, the ISO sponsored adult education classes and retreats on the East Coast. Delaney took on as a goal the founding of labor schools, such as Sealy had endorsed in conjunction with retreat movement, in every Jesuit school and parish across the nation. Several universities accordingly opened programs of social work; Fordham and Loyola in Chicago were among the first. The US Jesuit to gain the most celebrity in the area of labor relations, at least indirectly, was John M. Corridan (1911–84), whom superiors assigned to the Xavier Institute of Industrial Relations in Manhattan in 1946 and whose involvement with the International Longshoremen's Union became the inspiration for the priest-protagonist in Elia Kazan's 1954 Oscar-winning film *On the Waterfront.*

In 1943 the provincials decided to make the ISO more national by moving its offices from Manhattan to Saint Louis. Not only was Saint Louis geographically more central, it was home to the Sodality, the Jesuits' work in contact with the largest number of Catholic families. Even in Saint Louis, however, the ISO struggled. Its mandate to research and to organize, to exercise national influence and to stay rooted in local realities was sprawlingly ambitious. Most frustrating of all, it could not find the talent it needed to live up to its ambitions. To address this last problem, Leo Brown (1900–1978), a Harvard-trained economist with experience in labor organizing in Saint Louis, opened the Institute for Social Studies (ISS) in 1947. Its purpose was to train Jesuits in the social sciences and thus to give more scholarly heft to the ISO's organizing and teaching activities. But even with the provincials' endorsement, both the ISS and ISO were plagued by staffing problems, which were in part the result of provincial rivalries and institutional jealousies. The ISO ultimately felt compelled to cut its ties with the Sodality movement, shuttering its organizing activities in favor of research. The importance of the social apostolate was not in question, and the numbers of Jesuits with higher degrees in the social sciences increased. But the coordinated national program envisioned before the war was never realized. By mid-century, the social apostolate was a regional affair undertaken by provinces and institutions individually rather than in cooperation.

THE RACE QUESTION

Racial tensions and disparities in the United States were phenomena that arguably belonged in the ISO's wheelhouse but which were never fully brought into it. In 1935 an attempt to link anticommunism with antiracism at a West Baden meeting failed. While the attempt indicates general concern for the problem of race in America, that the problem took such regionally distinctive forms may best explain why the projects to address it emerge in connection to specific places and networks of specific people. The Jesuit who attained the highest profile in all this was John LaFarge, the same Jesuit who had advocated the grassroots approach to combating communism. LaFarge came from a privileged background. His father was the artist of the same name; and his mother, a convert to Catholicism, was the great great granddaughter of Benjamin Franklin. He graduated from Harvard University in 1901, after which he began studying for the priesthood at the University of Innsbruck. He was ordained and entered the Jesuits in 1905. Six years later, at age thirty-one, he began fifteen years of pastoral work in the parishes of southern Maryland, among them the congregation at Saint Peter Claver Church (to whom this book is dedicated). Jesuit annual catalogues from this segregated period distinguished between activities organized for Black people and those for whites, and the Jesuits assigned to each. La Farge was listed, for example, as moderating both the Black and the white branches of the Sacred Heart League, abbreviated in the Latin of these catalogues as "*foed. SS. Cord. alb. et nigrit.*" The assignment introduced him to rural African American communities and inspired in him a lifelong commitment to fighting African American poverty and improving race relations. He became a central figure in drawing the attention of the Catholic hierarchy and white faithful to the struggles of their Black coreligionists in the United States.

In May 1934, LaFarge founded the Catholic Interracial Council (CIC) of New York. The goal of "interracialism" was to transform Black Catholicism into one of the many cultural expressions that already composed "American Catholicism." The interracialists imagined that the Church could protect and further Black Catholic interests, both religious and civil, in ways akin to those of other ethnic groups. From this perspective, the challenges facing Black Catholics were distinctive from the challenges faced by, say, Irish and Polish Catholics, more in degree than in kind. By design the CICs' leadership was whiter and more clerical, and its operations were less activist than the older organization it ended up replacing, the Federated Colored Catholics. The CIC's goal was to provide Catholics, both Black and white, with a forum for the exchange of ideas about racial equality and civil rights in light of Catholic social teaching. Mutual understanding, it was assumed, would naturally lead to cooperation. The CIC in New York served as a model for similar councils in cities across the country. It also inspired such related organizations as the Catholic Intercollegiate Interracial Council in Philadelphia, which students at the Jesuits' Saint Joseph's College started in 1937 and five more Catholic colleges, both men's and women's, in the city joined.

In 1937 LaFarge wrote *Interracial Justice: A Study of the Catholic Doctrine of Race Relations* (later retitled *The Race Question*), in which he applied Catholic social teaching to the problems of race in the United States. Later that same decade, he directed for Pius XI the drafting of the never-promulgated encyclical *Humani generis unitas*, which condemned racism and anti-Semitism; and for Pius XII in 1939, he contributed to the drafting of *Sertum laetitiae*, which encouraged the US Jesuits to open their schools to African Americans. Three months before his death in 1963, he participated in the March on Washington and stood on the steps of the Lincoln Memorial behind Martin Luther King Jr.

Jesuit handling of school integration in Saint Louis provides another view on the order's engagement with the "race question." The Dutch émigré Ignatius Panken (1832–1906) had founded the Saint Elizabeth of Hungary Parish for African American Catholics (*pro nigrit.*, as the catalogues indicated) in Saint Louis in 1873. While the Oblate Sisters of Providence from Baltimore taught Black children at the grammar school there, the Jesuit schools in Saint Louis enrolled only white students. In fact, all Catholic schools in Saint Louis were segregated. In 1943 the pastor of Saint Elizabeth (and a frequent collaborator with LaFarge on race issues), William Markoe (1892–1969), began advocating for the matriculation of a Black woman at Saint Louis University. Overcoming the president's initial worry that desegregation would scare off donors and white students, William's brother John (1890–1967), also a Jesuit, persuaded the president to raise the possibility with faculty and alumni. The president circulated a survey among leading figures in the university community. Eager to spur the process forward, the Markoes passed the survey along to the city newspaper, thrusting the deliberations into the public eye. After an inconclusive meeting of the faculty, another Jesuit, Claude Heithaus (1898–1976), made the issue the theme of his Sunday sermon on February 11, 1944, at the university chapel, which he concluded by calling on the students to rise and to pledge, "Lord Jesus, we are sorry and ashamed for all the wrongs that white men have done to Your Colored children. We are firmly resolved never again to have any part in them, and to do everything in our power to prevent them. Amen." In consequence, the local archbishop admonished Heithaus as "a demagogue and a rabble-rouser," and the Jesuit university president ordered him to keep silent. Two months later, however, the university yielded to mounting pressure from the province, from the Jesuit authorities in Rome, and from the local press and announced the admission in the coming academic year of five Black students, two as undergraduates and three more as graduate students.

Such limited desegregation did not quell criticism, especially as the implications of this situation were increasingly understood to be national. George Dunne (1906–98), who earned a doctorate in international relations in 1944 from the University of Chicago and worked at the ISO, was abruptly reassigned to California during the Saint Louis controversy after he criticized the university's slow pace at desegregating. Dunne followed up with an essay in the influential Catholic lay magazine *Commonweal*, "The Short Case," in which he denounced segregation as a sinful breach of justice. The theologian John Courtney Murray (1904–67) wrote a petition from Woodstock in 1945 explaining that the integration of Jesuit schools was an obligation from principles of social justice, social charity, and supernatural charity. Black enrollment at Saint Louis slowly began to increase. Encouraged by the emerging outcome and despite the controversy, the archbishop called for the integration of all Catholic schools in 1947.

That same year, the Jesuits at Woodstock undertook a nationwide survey on race at Jesuit schools. Nearly all the schools responded. The results indicated that twenty-two of the thirty-four high schools were willing to admit Black students, but only half of them actually did, and some that had in that particular year had lost them already by midyear. The survey also indicated that of 82,000 college students, only 436 were Black; and four schools accounted for the majority of those enrollments: Saint Louis University, Fordham University, Seattle College, and Detroit College. The integration of Jesuit schools, the study concluded, had a long way to go.

Schools were the most obvious Jesuit institution needing integration, but they were not the only ones. In the 1950s, the New Orleans province made a concerted effort to desegregate all its institutions, even its own program of Jesuit training. In response to a letter on the social apostolate in 1949 from the superior general, Jean-Baptiste Janssens (1889–1964, r. 1946–64), the New Orleans province, which stretched from El Paso to Miami, undertook a study of economic disparities in its major cities. The results quantified—in terms of employment, wealth, and health—how significant the disparities were, especially between white and Black populations. Two provincials in tandem—Harry L. Crane

(1906–82) and William Crandell (1909–73)—committed themselves to tackling the race question in the province. Both recognized that a goal of unifying the province behind a policy of
integration needed to clear the hurdle of divisions among Jesuits
themselves toward race. A draft policy requiring the desegregation of Jesuit works as well as admission of Black men into
the order emerged in August 1952 from meetings held at Grand
Coteau in Louisiana. The plan was sent to Janssens, who endorsed it in January 1954, with revisions that tightened loopholes
and made the language less reluctant. The provincial ordered the
policy not to be made public but to be implemented institution by
institution: "We do not want headlines, but results." Results were
uneven. Spring Hill College in Mobile, Alabama, integrated almost at once. Loyola University in New Orleans admitted the first
Black student to its law school in 1952 but did not integrate its
undergraduate program until 1962, the year the local archbishop
mandated the desegregation of Catholic colleges in the archdiocese. Jesuit High School in New Orleans admitted eight Black
students in 1962, and the first two of them graduated in 1964.
The first Black man admitted to the novitiate in Grand Coteau,
Numa Rousseve (1939–, left 1965), arrived in 1956. He departed
the order shortly before he would have been ordained.

High levels of recruitment, burgeoning institutions, and
thoughtful, if not always successful, engagement in a range of
social and political challenges of great significance to Catholics in
America and around the globe contribute to the impression that
mid-century was a booming time for the Society in the United
States And indeed it was. Ascertaining the relation of this boom
time to the subsequent decades is no less a challenge for Jesuit
history than in Church history or American social history more
generally. Such an analysis gives the lie to the claim that hindsight
is twenty/twenty. It is to these following decades of turmoil that
we turn next, keeping as much of an eye on earlier roots as on the
novel developments of the second half of the twentieth century.

FURTHER READING

Primary Literature

Numerous Jesuits from early and mid-century produced memoirs. Three that bear on matters raised in this chapter are the following:

- LaFarge, John. *The Manner Is Ordinary*. New York: Harcourt, Brace, 1954. LaFarge also collaborated with the *Life* magazine photographer Margaret Bourke-White to produce *A Report on the American Jesuits* (New York: Farrar, Straus & Cudahy, 1956).
- Lord, Daniel. *Played by Ear*. Chicago: Loyola University Press, 1956.
- Ciszek, Walter. *With God in Russia*. New York: Harper One, 2017. Pennsylvania coal-town-born Walter Ciszek (1904–84) was assigned in 1938 to serve Eastern Catholics in Poland. As a result of the partition of Poland by Hitler's Germany and Stalin's Russia in 1939, he moved his ministry surreptitiously eastward until his arrest by Soviet police in Chusovoy, USSR, in 1941. He continued his priestly ministries while in prison and then in Siberian exile. In 1963 the Kennedy administration succeeded in negotiating his release. This volume, along with a companion volume *He Leadeth Me*, is his memoir of imprisonment; together, they have risen to the level of spiritual classics.

The diocesan priest John A. Ryan wrote two works that influenced American Jesuits and represented strains of Catholic thought that inspired much Jesuit activity in the early twentieth century: *A Living Wage* (New York: Grosset & Dunlap, 1906); and *Distributive Justice: The Right and Wrong of Our Present Distribution of Wealth* (New York: Macmillan, 1916).

Institute of Social Order, ed. *Social Orientations*. Chicago: Loyola University Press, 1956. The Institute of Social Order at Saint Louis University produced this college textbook to support "an integrated course in the social sciences" for "all who are interested in understanding and applying the papal social programs." The book offers a helpful example of and view onto the Jesuit response to the calls from Rome in the middle third of the century to pursue a Christian social order in the United States. Leading Jesuit social scientists of the day, led by Leo Brown, contributed: Albert S. Foley (1912–90), who as a sociologist at Spring Hill College became an active participant in the civil rights movement, on race relations; "labor priest" Mortimer H. Gavin (1914–84), who founded the Institute of Industrial Relations for the Boston Archdiocese in 1962, on labor–management relations; Philip S. Land (1911–94), who later taught economics at the Gregorian University in Rome, on a living wage; and John L. Thomas (1910–81), on the welfare state and safety nets, among others.

Secondary Literature

Anderson, R. Bentley. *Black, White, and Catholic: New Orleans Interracialism, 1947–1956.* Nashville: Vanderbilt University Press, 2005. This civil rights history is fascinating, for several reasons: Anderson takes the understudied period antedating the better-known national protests of the 1960s; he analyzes Catholicism's ambivalent contributions to the early history; and he examines to fine granularity the multiple positions on race within Black and white communities, sometimes working together, sometimes cooperatively, and sometimes against one another. The volume puts the Jesuit part(s) in all this in a larger, regional context, of which the Jesuits are themselves only one part: the efforts of the New Orleans province to desegregate its works and the work of the Jesuit sociologist Joseph Fichter on behalf of Catholic interracialism based at Loyola University in New Orleans.

Enochs, Ross. *The Jesuit Mission to the Lakota Sioux: A Study of Pastoral Ministry, 1886–1945.* Kansas City: Sheed & Ward, 1996. The author offers a sympathetic account of Jesuit outreach to the Lakota and their treatment of Native cultural and religious practices.

Gruenberg, Gladys W. *Labor Peacemaker: The Life and Works of Father Leo C. Brown, SJ.* Saint Louis: Institute of Jesuit Sources, 1981. This work introduces the reader to the Jesuit attempt to bring Catholic social thought to bear on the world of industry and labor through the biography of Leo Brown, SJ. The pope's exhortation to US Jesuits to

Christian social order" in their country was the launch-
st of Brown's assignments and accomplishments. Brown
the Institute of Social Sciences and Institute of Social
...mu-century (see *Social Orientations* above).

McDonough, Peter. *Men Astutely Trained: A History of the Jesuits in the American Century*. New York: Free Press, 1992. McDonough is a retired professor of political science. While the work's title suggests a general history, *Men Astutely Trained* is at its most interesting when McDonough focuses on "the social apostolate" and Jesuit interest in the social sciences in the first two thirds of the century. The work is most useful when studied from the index backward to specific topics in the text.

Southern, David W. *John Lafarge and the Limits of Catholic Interracialism, 1911–1963*. Baton Rouge: Louisiana State University Press, 1996. The biography offers insight into the leading proponent among Jesuits of racial equality for African Americans in the Church and civil society in the early and mid–twentieth century. Southern highlights Lafarge's accomplishments but also draws attention to what he sees as an underlying paternalism in Lafarge's gradualist approach.

5

Upheaval, 1960–2000

T**HE JESUIT SUPERIOR GENERAL** Pedro Arrupe (1907–91, r. 1965–83) remarked in 1977 that the order was living through a period more challenging than any since the Suppression itself. A sense of tumult in the late twentieth century was felt not only in the order but also across the Church and civil society. On the Church's side, the Second Vatican Council stirred excitement worldwide among Catholics and non-Catholics alike. It sat from 1962 to 1965, but its roots reached back generations. On the secular side, powerful political and social movements—the rise of second-wave feminism, the civil rights movement at home and processes of decolonization abroad, and opposition to the Vietnam War worldwide, for example—were stirring up all kinds of change in the 1960s and 1970s. These highlights coincided with serious change in religious practice in the United States: Numerous shifting indicators—for example, habits of service attendance, participation in religious education programs, rates of baptism as well as of church weddings and of religious funerals, recruitment for and retention in the ministry—indicate a general religious decline in this period. Additional changes were distinctive to Catholicism, some also indicative of growth: its demographic center was shifting from northeast to southwest, large portions of its population with European roots moved into the middle and upper classes and relocated from the cities into the suburbs, and the proportion of adherents with non-European backgrounds increased. Many of these trends continue to the present day. The aim of this chapter is to draw attention to how these trends in church and society affected the US Jesuits and how the order reacted, even as the era's nearness to the present makes historical assessment necessarily incomplete and tentative.

DEMOGRAPHIC DROPS
AND SPIRITUAL SURGES

The Society of Jesus reached its largest size in the United States in 1965 with 8,393 members. Ten years later, US numbers had fallen 25 percent, to 6,220. A similar decline was experienced worldwide. Novitiate classes decreased in size, and the departures of vowed Jesuits from the order increased. Some separations gained national attention: the abrupt departure of a sitting provincial in 1968 to civilly marry a divorcée, for example, was covered by the *New York Times*. The Seminar on Jesuit Spirituality, a research group founded by the provincials in 1969 to address matters of spiritual concern to Jesuits, dedicated an issue of its journal *Studies* to the topic of declining membership in 1977. Joseph M. Becker (1908–2001), a labor economist trained at Columbia University, wrote the principal article. He compared the demographic deterioration of the Society with an economic depression. The Society's troubles, he opined, resulted from the long neglect of serious problems, but quantitative decline was the necessary precondition for long-term qualitative improvement. He speculated that cultural forces long at play within Western society and newly dominant were challenging the Jesuit order, like the Church as a whole. He identified several general cultural shifts as particularly relevant: from the objective to the subjective, from the absolute to the relative, from the sacral to the secular, and from the institutional to the individual.

Other Seminar members responded with further explanations, generally of two kinds. The one scrutinized developments in the

Church. The philosopher Robert Harvanek (1917–96), for example, proposed that the Thomistic revival—a philosophical movement that had dominated Catholic thought from Pope Leo XIII's
Pastor aeternus in 1879 until Vatican II—had run its course and
was no longer able to sustain the Jesuit vision and activity that
had driven it forward in the preceding century. The theologian
David Fleming (1935–2011) identified a transition in his discipline over the preceding decades "from an objective set of tradi-
tionally expressed expectations and memorizable formulations to
an open-ended challenge to personal commitment aimed at living
with the implications of what one knows, and to seeking value
and worth in what one is and expects."

Another kind of explanation focused on the inadequacies
of Jesuit training. William Connolly (1925–2013) and William
Barry (1930–2020), the codirectors of a new center for training in
spiritual direction in Boston, explained,

> The typical formation program was inflexible, narrowly con-
> ceived, and distinctly lacking in ability to prepare men to meet
> the conditions in which the '60s and '70s would require them
> to live and work. It did not, for instance, encourage the per-
> sonal suppleness and openness to others' views and feelings that
> would enable them to work as team minsters; it did not prepare
> them to collaborate as peers with the women who made up
> more than half the ministerial force of the American Church; it
> prepared them to teach the laity, but not to act as co-workers
> for the Kingdom with them; it did little to form them to a ma-
> ture personal prayer that would sustain them in their personal
> and apostolic lives when they lived and worked outside the field
> of force provided by strong institutional structures; it did not
> encourage them to integrate their aggressivity into their spiri-
> tual lives; it did too much to encourage them to see life through
> institutional eyes and too little to enable them to see and re-
> spond to the varied and rapidly changing non-institutional
> needs of God's people.

They concluded that the demographic upheaval within the order should be taken as "a salvific opportunity" to replace the "religious weakness of the Society of Jesus as it entered the '60s" with a vibrant religious community shaped by a spiritual and personalist revival.

The respondents were unanimous on a key point that informed an emerging strategy within the Jesuit leadership. The response to the declining number of Jesuits should not try to regain "lost vocations" but rather to invigorate the spiritual and personal lives of those who remained and joined fresh. This reform's expressed aim was to improve the quality of the order's service to the Church. What none of the respondents seemed to anticipate, however, was that the quantitative decline was to continue— as across seminaries and religious congregations in the United States—for decades to come. A half century that began with the expectation of Jesuit membership in the United States ascending into five digits ended with the outlook that it could fall to three. Assessing, recalibrating, and amending the commitments made on the mistaken assumption that the earlier growth was sustainable thus emerged as major challenges, challenges continuing to the present day.

The effort to invigorate Jesuit life found encouragement from multiple sides. The Council's call for religious renewal through a process of *ressourcement*—a return to historical, spiritual sources—and *aggiornamento*—a bringing up to date—inspired much self-scrutiny and experimentation during the late twentieth century. All four general congregations in the late twentieth century occupied themselves with the call to renewal, especially the first two, the thirty-first (1964–65) and the thirty-second (1974–75). Jesuit engagement with *ressourcement* had actually already been under way for several generations thanks to the work of the Jesuit Historical Institute (IHSI) in Rome. Its task was the editing and publication of documents related to the founding and early history of the Jesuits. George E. Ganss (1905–2000) founded the Institute of Jesuit Sources (IJS) in Saint Louis in 1961. The IJS strove to put in the hands of every Jesuit foundational documents

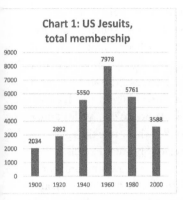

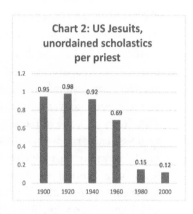

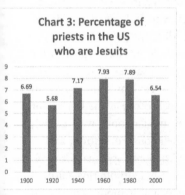

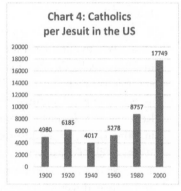

FIGURE 5.1 Jesuit membership: demographic change in the twentieth century. Sources: *The Catholic Directory* and Jesuit province catalogues, 1901, 1921, 1941, 1961, 1981, 2001.

that had earlier been, with few exceptions, available to them only in abbreviated and Latin forms. Ganss's successor, John W. Padberg (1926–2021), sustained and expanded this program; and the quality of the historical analysis reached a high point in *The First Jesuits* by John W. O'Malley (1927–2022) in 1995.

The scholarly work of the IHSI had practical effects on Jesuit spirituality. One marker of that development was a new format in which the Spiritual Exercises were offered to retreatants. Up to that point, Jesuits customarily offered the Exercises—the thirty-day sequence of meditations developed by Saint Ignatius and the centerpiece of Jesuit spirituality—in a preached format. Historical research was uncovering, and underscoring, that Saint Ignatius and the early Jesuits had offered the Exercises through a course of one-to-one conversations with a retreatant. In the English-speaking world, the tertianship at Saint Beuno's in Wales under Paul Kennedy (1903–88, in office 1958–74) became the epicenter for the spread of the individually directed Spiritual Exercises. The heart of tertianship, the final stage of Jesuit training and for a priest coming immediately or soon after his ordination, was, and still is, the undertaking of the full Spiritual Exercises. The Guelph Centre of Spirituality in Ontario, founded in 1969 by Canadian Jesuits John J. English (1924–2004), who had completed his tertianship under Kennedy six years earlier, and John Veltri (1933–2008), was the first institutional foothold in North America for the individually directed Exercises. US disciples of the renewed spirituality, many of them Kennedy's tertians, rallied around newly established spiritual centers: in Boston, at the Center for Religious Development (where Barry and Connolly were based); in Saint Louis, at the Institute of Religious Formation; and in Wernersville, Pennsylvania, at the Center for Spiritual Growth. These centers dedicated themselves not only to offering spiritual and retreat direction in the new personalist mode but also to training new directors. These trainees came to include not only Jesuits but also other priests and religious, laymen and women, and non-Catholics.

Changes in Jesuit Formation

These new insights into Jesuit history and spirituality guided the order's governance as it overhauled the order's program of training. Initially the provincials hoped to develop a reformed training program with a working group whose membership would be fully representative of the order in the United States. This group convened at Santa Clara University in August 1966 as the Conference on the Total Development of the Jesuit Priest. The conference served as a clearinghouse for ideas of reform. It produced six volumes of proceedings, whose contents touched on every aspect of Jesuit life. The conference became notorious for raising a possible "third way" of living chastity situated between married life and consecrated celibacy. Father Arrupe intervened quickly to affirm that nothing from the recent Second Vatican Council offered the "basis for 'a third way.'" In the end, even the body of serious reflection recorded in the proceedings was too diffuse, and the effect of the conference was inspirational rather than legislative.

The changes to Jesuit formation implemented over the next decade fell into three categories, at least the first two of which were characteristic worldwide: a heightened individualization of the training process, a reduction in the formal structures of religious life, and renegotiated relationships between formational institutions and related non-Jesuit institutions. Howard Gray (1930–2018), himself a product of the Kennedy tertianship, led the way in implementing reform along these lines at the joint Chicago–Detroit novitiate, newly relocated to Berkley, Michigan, in 1971. The other novitiates, most of which had moved from rural to urban settings by 1980, followed suit. As Saint Ignatius's idea of "experiments"—a set of short-term, intense assignments for the novices and a distinctive component of the Jesuit noviceship—was recovered from generations of neglect, larger portions of the two-year program took place away from the novitiate precincts. The novice's day now comprised more unstructured time for prayer and reflection, the reduction of required and standardized devotions, and communal prayer as reformed by the Council's new liturgical directives. Personalist psychological insight was also more robustly incorporated into the guidance a novice received from his novice director. As might be expected in a period of rapid change, not all changes were implemented with adequate preparation, equal deftness, or ultimate success. Still, the energy invested was enormous, and optimism that things were heading in the right direction was boundless.

The later stages of formation were reformed in analogous ways. Several stages of academic work followed the novitiate. All were revised. Juniorates, where Jesuits received a post-high-school introduction to the humanities, were disbanded as novices increasingly arrived with college degrees in hand. Students of philosophy and of theology had commonly lived and studied together. Now the philosophy programs were relocated to Jesuit universities, where scholastics worked for degrees alongside lay peers. By 2000, three such programs were (and still are) in place, at Fordham University, Loyola University Chicago, and Saint Louis University. The theology faculties, while retaining their autonomy as free-standing institutions, moved into cities. Characteristic of the successful transitions at the time was the move of Alma College, the theology school of the California and Oregon provinces, from isolation in the foothills of the Santa Cruz Mountains to the urban eastern shore of the San Francisco Bay, in 1969. Successfully guiding the transition were two successive rectors, Harry T. Corcoran (1909–97), a dogmatic theologian trained in Rome, and Michael J. Buckley (1931–2019), a philosophical theologian trained at Chicago. The school, renamed the Jesuit School of Theology at Berkeley (JSTB, and today affiliated with Santa Clara University), joined the Graduate Theological Union, a consortium of divinity schools, including several sponsored by Protestant denominations and other Catholic religious orders. Scholastics could also take courses at the University of California.

A contemporaneous failure was the attempt to do something similar with the country's oldest and most prestigious theology faculty, Woodstock College. It relocated in 1969 from rural Maryland to the Upper West Side of Manhattan. Acting ever more in concert, the US provincials, however, had sketched a plan to reduce the number of theology schools by two according to a set of standards they expressed in the so-called Fordyce Statement. An initial vote of the provincials recommended the closing of the theology schools in Weston, Massachusetts, and Saint Louis. But a sluggishness in Woodstock's embrace of the new standards, a lingering ambivalence over the benefits of the move to Manhattan

(New Haven had been also considered), internal tensions over community life that became public in a major magazine article, and some last-minute lobbying on behalf of certain schools led the provincials by a slim majority and at the last minute to change their decision and recommend the closure of Woodstock instead of Weston. Arrupe accepted that recommendation in 1972. By 2000, JSTB and Weston (at that point relocated to Cambridge, Massachusetts, and now the School of Theology and Ministry at Boston College) were the two remaining theology faculties in the United States. Scholastics now studied theology alongside a growing proportion of lay students, who were pursuing advanced degrees with the hope of serving the Church in ways, such as seminary teaching, previously reserved to clerics.

The difference between the systems of formation in 1950 and 2000 is quite striking. Jesuits from both eras shared the Spiritual Exercises but were making them in sharply different ways, preached in 1950 and individually directed in 2000. The model eighteen-year-old novice of mid-century who had been reared in a practicing Catholic family, had graduated from a Jesuit high school, and was admitted on a local rector's good word was re-placed by a man averaging in his mid-twenties, of unpredictable Catholic upbringing, and rigorously screened, spiritually, psycho-logically, and medically. Centerpieces of the educational training following vows were still philosophy and theology, but a stan-dardized neo-Thomistic curriculum taught in Latin was replaced with a range of theological approaches. Study of, let alone in, the sacred languages became rare. In the classroom, scholastics were indistinguishable in dress from their lay fellow students, and faculties developed new curricula to accommodate a growing contingent of lay students not seeking, or eligible for, ordination. Regency, the two- or three-year work practicum situated between the two periods of academic study, was as distinctive to Jesuit training as ever. But even when undertaken in the customary form at a high school, the new Jesuit regent was commonly assigned alone in 2000, not as in the past in double-digit cohorts. The new regent was also inured to a new working relationship with laymen

and laywomen that was to become the standard across aposto-
lates and beyond ordination: to work with them as colleagues
and mentors, and to report to them as supervisors. Foreign-born
Jesuits, a small portion of novitiate entrances at mid-century,
were now coming from outside Europe, notably from Southeast
Asia and Latin America. By the time a US Jesuit had reached final vows, he likely had substantive international experience, less
commonly in Europe, as in the past, than in the Global South.
The cultural gap between the Jesuit-in-training of 2000 and of
1950 was surely larger than any generational gap since—to use
Arrupe's measure in 1977—the Suppression itself.

THE SCHOOLS

The Jesuits' educational commitment to the laity at the universities and the high schools likewise underwent great change. The
quandaries the universities faced were not entirely unlike those
in the preceding century: how to sustain a curriculum true to a
venerable Jesuit educational vision and suitable to contemporary
circumstances, how to cultivate the faculty as both teachers and
scholars, and how to win recognition of the quality of this education within the Catholic community and beyond it. Even before the
turmoil of the 1960s, the pointed criticism of American Catholic
intellectual mediocrity, even apathy, by an eminent historian at
the Catholic University of America, Monsignor John Tracy Ellis,
in 1955 had turned up the heat on seminaries and universities
across the country. In reaction, the University of Notre Dame's
legendary president Theodore Hesburgh, CSC, sponsored discussions among Catholic educational leaders on how to break out of
what Ellis had called a "self-imposed ghetto mentality," invigorate Catholic intellectual life, and reform Catholic higher education. The discussions culminated in 1967 with a new statement of
purpose. In its preamble, the so-called Land O'Lakes Statement
articulated three necessary characteristics of a Catholic university:
"a strong commitment to and concern for academic excellence";
"true autonomy and academic freedom" from any authority

"external to the academic community itself"; and a "community of scholars, in which Catholicism is perceptively present and effectively operative." Land O'Lakes' ambitious vision created the springboard from which Catholic research universities, including several Jesuit ones, emerged in the last quarter of the century. At the same time, many observers of and stakeholders in Catholic higher education identified in the preamble an irresolvable tension between Catholic identity and modern ideas of academic freedom. Under that tension and given the sea change in Catholic practice sketched at the outset of this chapter, how to ensure a "community of scholars," in which Catholicism is "perceptively present and effectively operative" became a vexing challenge for university leadership and a contested issue within the order and the Church. Pope John Paul II's document on Catholic institutions of higher learning in 1990, *Ex corde Ecclesiae*, brought only partial resolution to the problem. Accompanying this unease was another over how the Jesuits themselves understood their apostolic purpose at the universities in light of the changing needs, expectations, and characteristics of the schools and their clientele. Even allowing for the variations and exceptions that nineteenth- and early twentieth-century examples testify to, the much discussed, idealized model of an apostolic complex staffed by Jesuits and serving the educational and pastoral needs of an otherwise underserved, local, urban Catholic population of European background at the behest of the local bishop was no longer possible; what now would replace it?

Hand-in-hand came developments in how the Jesuit universities operated as institutions. As the universities grew in size and complexity, the customary form of governance that put decision-making in the hands of local rectors and their Jesuit advisers proved inadequate. Alongside such operational concerns, a general reassessment of traditional apostolic commitments taking place within the order was fueling, especially among younger Jesuits, a dissatisfaction over the schools as a priority for the order and a dismay at the quality of the religious life of Jesuits at these institutions. In this ferment, the universities underwent a restructuring of their basic relationship with the order. The signal development was the process of "separate incorporation" that began at Saint Louis University in 1967 and spread within five years to nearly all other Jesuit universities. Separate incorporation entailed that the universities, as public trusts, become civilly independent from the order: the offices of university president and local religious superior were filled by different people (a practice already with some precedent by this point) and through different processes, corporate oversight of the universities was placed in the hands of increasingly lay boards, and the provincial's and local superior's authority in management decisions was yielded to these boards and their administrative appointees. Reworked articles of incorporation resulted in significant transfers of property from the provinces to the schools. Internal to the university, leading offices in the administration, previously restricted to Jesuits, were opened to non-Jesuits; and lay faculty, in most schools long outnumbering the Jesuits, was brought into collaborative processes of decision-making. Under this new dispensation, the University of Detroit–Mercy hired the first non-Jesuit president of a Jesuit university, Maureen Fay, OP, in 1983, and John J. DeGioia became the first lay president in 2001 at Georgetown University. (As of the summer of 2022, at twenty-eight Jesuit colleges and universities, there are five Jesuit presidents, and six of the lay presidents are women.)

The high schools underwent similar institutional changes, but the struggle to identify their defining characteristic as "Jesuit" worked itself out more smoothly. The Jesuit Education Association sponsored a study in 1964 to determine the effectiveness of Jesuit high schools in the Christian formation of their student bodies. It commissioned Harvard-trained sociologist Joseph Fichter (1908–94) to direct the evaluation. The results were startling: Jesuit secondary education, according to the final report *Send Us a Boy . . . Get Back a Man*, might be highly regarded for enhancing students' social status but could not be credited with fostering their long-term religious commitment. Putting the blame on the Jesuits themselves, the Fichter Report was a shot across the bow of the order's most esteemed work. It also fueled the growing disparagement of the Society's high schools from younger Jesuits as little more than greenhouses for "bourgeois Catholicism."

In reaction to *Send Us a Boy*, the provincials founded the Jesuit Secondary Education Association (JSEA), whose task was to develop the religious dimension within the educational mission of the high schools. JSEA's focus came to encompass attentiveness not simply to the development of a curriculum but also to the training of administration and faculty in a freshly envisioned, distinctively Jesuit pedagogy. That pedagogy, shaped by the renewed Ignatian spirituality, was articulated in terms of the intellectual and moral education of "the whole person" and service learning for the common good with heightened attentiveness to the problems of poverty and social marginalization. The robustness of the new ideal of Jesuit education also opened up the possibility of new kinds of educational enterprises.

Two such enterprises began as solitary efforts and then became models for national programs. The first was a program of primary schooling founded to serve socially marginalized and educationally underserved urban populations. It began with one province's commitment to a particular parochial school in New York City in 1971. Named after that first project, the Nativity-style school led to a national coalition of middle schools, serving low-income families, primarily in Hispanic and African American urban communities. The other began as a single secondary school in a Latino quarter of Chicago in 1996. Cristo Rey Jesuit School's founding director, John P. Foley (1939–), developed relationships with city businesses that provided a basis for the school's funding and curricular internships for students. New Cristo Rey–style schools became a main feature of the Jesuits' national efforts in secondary education. The success of its work-study model led other Catholic educational interests to adopted it as well: today other organizations and dioceses sponsor two-thirds of the schools in the national Cristo Rey network.

The changes in the schools, at all levels, over the course of the late twentieth century draw attention to the intersection of

influences shaping Jesuit commitments in the period, even beyond the schools. The influences have been of two kinds: one
set encompasses ideals and aspirations, some quite old and often enhanced or revised by the ecclesial documents issued in the
1960s and 1970s. The second set was of a pressing practical sort:
The decreasing membership of the order meant ever fewer Jesuits
were available to staff these works, and a changing laity—some
more empowered, some less churched—necessarily meant that
different forms of collaboration and service had to emerge. Only
with these forces taken in conjunction are the differences between
the schools of the 1950s and those of the 2000s intelligible.

Learned Activities

The Jesuit commitment to the schools as educational institutions
in this period continued, as in the past, to be complemented by
the commitment to scholarship. In the middle and late twentieth
century, there were more US Jesuits of national and international
standing in both sacred and secular disciplines than ever before,
and younger Jesuits were increasingly encouraged to pursue higher
degrees not at ecclesiastical institutions but at secular research
universities of the highest rank. By way of example and drawing
from across disciplines, among the most significant contributors
to theological reflection in this period was the moralist Richard
A. McCormick (1922–2000). His regular contribution to the
journal *Theological Studies*, "Moral Notes," analyzed contemporary moral questions according to the standards of traditional
Catholic moral thought. He attracted attention for applying the
tradition to the era's latest ethical challenges, such as surrogate
motherhood, euthanasia, and patients' rights. Joseph A. Fitzmyer
(1920–2016), a biblical scholar who earned scholarly renown for
his work on the Dead Sea Scrolls and the Gospel of Luke, served
on the Pontifical Biblical Commission and as president of the US
Catholic Biblical Association. George W. MacRae (1928–85),
who was interim dean of Harvard Divinity School and its first
Roman Catholic head ever when he died, had established himself

as a leading scholar of Gnosticism and early Christian theology with his translation and interpretation of the Coptic manuscripts discovered in Egypt in 1957. J. Quentin Lauer (1917–97) earned regard as a Hegel scholar for, as he put it, trying to do for Hegel what Aquinas had done for Aristotle. The theologian Walter J. Burghardt (1914–2008) was acclaimed as one of the nation's greatest preachers of any denomination and dedicated the last decades of his life to invigorating Catholic preaching through priest retreats.

In the secular disciplines, Walter J. Ong (1912–2003) was a scholar of language and its history at Saint Louis University. His 1982 article "Orality and Literacy" remains four decades later a touchstone in its field. The work of the historian John W. Witek (1933–2010) on Catholicism in seventeenth- and eighteenth-century East Asia was highly respected at home, where the American Historical Association lauded it upon his death as "formidable scholarship," and in China, where it circulated in Mandarin translation. Timothy J. Toohig (1928–2001) earned an international reputation as a physicist, with a decades-long appointment at the Fermi National Accelerator Laboratory near Chicago and with contributions to the Superconducting Super Collider Project in Dallas and to the Large Hadron Collider at CERN, the European Particle Physics Laboratory in Geneva. George D. Ruggieri (1925–87), a marine biologist, attracted national attention for his work *The Healing Sea* (1967), in which he described the oceans as vast untapped pharmacies. He served as director of the New York Aquarium and Osborn Laboratories of Marine Sciences from 1976 to 1987.

Foreign Jesuits, as in eras past, were also able to make new homes in the United States. Among the most eminent of such scholars was the Hungarian canonist Ladislaus Orsy (1921–), a refugee from Communist Hungary who taught at Fordham, Catholic, and Georgetown universities after his arrival in the United States from Rome in 1966. Others found homes at secular institutions. The French anthropologist Michel de Certeau (1925–86) worked at the University of California, San Diego; from 1978 to

1984, the Canadian theologian Bernard J. F. Lonergan (1904–84) taught at Harvard, as well as Boston College, from 1971 to 1983; and the German Islamicist Gerhard Böwering (1939–) made his scholarly career at the University of Pennsylvania (1975–84) and Yale University (1985–2019).

Other institutional connections were emerging for research, especially in the social sciences and with an eye to public policy implications. At a UN ceremony in 1971, the Jesuits and the National Conference of Catholic Bishops jointly established the Center of Concern in Washington, a think tank for studying issues of development and peace from a global perspective. Its first directors were the Canadian William F. Ryan (1925–2017) and the Oregonian Peter J. Henriot (1936–). Analogous efforts to inspire public policy based on sound scholarship were plentiful, such as the work on migration and human rights by the moral theologian David Hollenbach (1942–) and the sociologist Rick Ryscavage (1945–2019).

Jesuits were also undertaking learned reflection in journals, especially with an eye to enriching broader conversation within Catholic America and worldwide. Three very different periodicals, for example, came to dominate Jesuit publishing activity in the second half of the twentieth century, all of them founded in the first half. The oldest aimed itself at the broadest readership: Based in New York City, the news magazine *America* published articles on political and cultural topics from a Catholic perspective. Its editorial staff addressed controversial issues, criticizing Catholic Senator Joseph McCarthy's red-baiting in the 1950s and later sponsoring discussions on contested issues within the Church, such as the prohibition on the use of artificial contraception by the married and the ordination of women. Founded in 1940, *Theological Studies* harnessed the Jesuit theology faculties to produce the nation's first scholarly journal of Catholic theology and remains arguably the most important such journal in the English language. The third, *Review for Religious*, published in Saint Louis from 1942 to 2012, featured articles on vowed religious life in all forms—male and female, contemplative and active—to address themes such as prayer and spirituality, challenges of the common life, and issues of canonical concern.

RELIGIOUS LIBERTY, ECUMENISM, AND INTERRELIGIOUS DIALOGUE

Of the theological issues deliberated at the Vatican Council, religious liberty and ecumenism were two issues of special interest to US participants. The United States was distinctive among Western nations in the religious diversity of its population and the constitutional protections afforded religious liberty. Religious diversity and religious liberty had had centuries-long implications for the American Catholic minority, no less than for Jesuit life and work. Two American Jesuits made significant contributions to theological reflection on these two values, as well as to their endorsement by the Council. John Courtney Murray (1904–67) worked to reconcile Catholicism with American notions of religious pluralism and religious freedom, and Gustave Weigel (1906–64) worked to develop Catholic participation in the ecumenical movement. Both were on the faculty at Woodstock, and Murray recruited Weigel to be the staff specialist at *Theological Studies* for Protestant theology. In addition to their academic theological work, they gained national reputations just before the Council with books aimed at broad readerships: Murray's *We Hold These Truths: Catholic Reflections on the American Proposition* (1960) was a collection of essays on the tensions between religious faith and public life. Weigel coauthored a reflection on Catholic–Protestant relations with a leading Presbyterian theologian who later served as an official observer at the Council, Robert McAfee Brown: *An American Dialogue: A Protestant Looks at Catholicism and a Catholic Looks at Protestantism* (1960). Despite having been prohibited from publishing on church–state relations by the Holy See in 1954, Murray came to the Council as an expert theologian of the archbishop of New York, Francis Cardinal Spellman. Weigel participated as an expert on ecumenical questions and as an adviser to Augustine Cardinal Bea at the Secretariat for the Promotion

FIGURE 5.2   John Courtney Murray and Avery Dulles, early 1960s. Dulles (1918–2008), the son of John Foster Dulles and a convert to Catholicism from Presbyterianism, was a theologian on the faculty of Woodstock College from 1960 to 1974, and thus Murray's colleague there for eight years. In 1975 the Catholic Theological Society of America elected Dulles to a term as president. Several Jesuits have held that office over the years, including Richard McCormick and John H. Wright (1922–2009) before him, and Michael Buckley and Roger Haight (1936–) after him. He served on the International Theological Commission, an advisory body to the Sacred Congregation for the Doctrine of the Faith. He was a Catholic signatory to the document "Evangelicals and Catholics Together" in 1994, which expressed a desire to align the two religious groups on matters of shared, social, and cultural interest. Pope John Paul II created Dulles a cardinal in 2001. Source: John Courtney Murray and Avery Dulles (n.d., n.l.), photograph by Thomas N. Lorsung, BFCSC, John Courtney Murray, SJ, Papers, box 25, folder 1218.

of Christian Unity. In the end, ideas advocated for by both men found approval at the Council.

The Council's decrees bolstered Jesuit engagement in ecumenical and interfaith dialogues. Weigel's own student, John Long (1925–2005); Michael Fahey (1933–), a former doctoral student of Joseph Ratzinger; Edward Kilmartin (1923–94) at the Weston School of Theology; Robert Taft (1932–2018), an American at the Pontifical Oriental Institute; and the patristic scholar Brian Daley (1940–) actively participated in the late-twentieth-century Orthodox-Catholic Dialogue. Avery Dulles (1918–2008), Joseph Fitzmyer, and Jared Wicks (1929–) were participants in the Lutheran–Catholic Dialogue and contributed to the Joint Declaration on the Doctrine of Justification, signed by Catholic and Lutheran leaders in 1999. Privileged among all such dialogues was that with the Jews: Donald Clifford (1929–2009) as long-time head of the Institute for Jewish–Catholic Relations at Saint Joseph's University and James Bernauer (1944–) at Boston College through his studies of Catholic anti-Semitism contributed to Jewish–Catholic relations. The theologian Raymond Helmick (1931–2016) made interreligious understanding practical: he worked for years on conflict resolution, or "conflict transformation" as he called it, between Catholic and Protestant paramilitaries in Northern Ireland and between Muslims and Jews in the Middle East. He also served as an election observer in the Kurdish controlled area of northern Iraq in 1992 and participated in prisoner release talks in the Balkans in 1999.

Other Jesuits took up the challenge of working with world religions. Francis X. Clooney (1950–), a leading figure in the study of Hinduism and in the 2010s the director of the Center for the Study of World Religions at Harvard, highlighted the different contours guiding interfaith dialogue: All Christians must confront the challenge posed, on the one hand, by Christ's mandate to the Church to "proclaim the Gospel" and, on the other hand, the necessary openness on the part of participants to "re-imagin[ing] their] religious identities in a context of dialog." Even as Jesuits' global extension put them in contact with the practice of many religions in their cultures of origins, Clooney pointed to a distinctively American dimension of this dialogue in that "the so-called 'world religions' are now also 'American religions'" due to the waves of immigrants to the United States from all corners of the globe. In the context of interreligious dialogue, Robert Edward Kennedy (1933–) earned recognition as a Zen roshi; and Thomas Michel (1941–), with a doctorate in Islamic Studies from Chicago, taught in Indonesia and served as head of the Office for Relations with Muslims under Pope John Paul II.

"In the Pews" and "at the Prie-Dieu"

These activities—in the classroom and working on ecumenism and the interfaith dialogue—certainly had implications for the life of ordinary Catholics, but at a step removed from those most obvious religious activities that take place "in the pew" and "at the prie-dieu," that is, public and private prayer. While harder to characterize and less centrally organized, Jesuits' direct work with Catholics on Sundays in church and at prayer continued through the last half of the century. In 1975 the Jesuits sponsored twenty-nine retreat houses and worked pastorally at scores of parishes and campus ministries, some sponsored by the Society, others not. Even as many of the most popular devotions of the nineteenth and early twentieth centuries struggled to articulate their purpose from the 1960s on, the Sacred Heart Radio still broadcast nation-wide and continued into the current century. Pedro Arrupe gave special endorsement to the Apostleship of Prayer (since 2010, the Pope's Worldwide Prayer Network), an international movement founded by French scholastics in 1844 and associated with the Sacred Heart devotion. In the United States, men continued to be assigned to foster it.

Jesuits also contributed to new movements originating outside their own ambit. One such movement was the charismatic renewal. Jesuit engagement had, as social scientists would put it, both first- and second-order dimensions; that is, Jesuits both did it and wrote about it. The charismatic renewal formally took root in the United States in 1967 at Duquesne University, a school founded by the Congregation of the Holy Spirit. A small number of Jesuits fostered Pentecostal practices of prayer at parishes and universities. Harold S. Cohen (1928–2001), for example, first ran Pentecostal prayer meetings at Loyola University in New Orleans and then founded the Catholic Charismatic Renewal of New

Orleans. "Charismatic" movements were often cast in opposition to hierarchical Christianity. Working to stem that potential in the movement, Cohen regularly encouraged his fellow charismatics to have "complete openness with your bishop." With similar concerns, Donald L. Gelpi (1934–2011) published the first systematic analysis of Pentecostalism in 1971, comparing it with other "devout movements" in Church history such as Catharism and Jansenism. The charismatic renewal attracted enough attention in the 1970s within the order that the theologian John Haughey (1930–2019) interviewed forty Jesuits active in the movement for *Studies in the Spirituality of Jesuits* in 1973. His questions delved more into what "the Pentecostal thing" might do for the Society than what the Society might do for it. Robert L. Faricy (1926–2022), a professor of spiritual theology at the Gregorian University in Rome and at Marquette University in Milwaukee, studied and ran workshops on the movement.

The Jesuits are also famous for their use of the arts to engage believers "in the pews" and "at the prie-dieu," and to evangelize. The fine art they have produced and commissioned is generally less, and less celebrated, after the Suppression than before. In the United States, the best-known Jesuit contributions to the fine arts are in architecture. Many cities across the nation can boast Jesuit edifices that are eye-catching and authentic expressions of local communities' religious loyalties and yearnings. Like most American church architecture, these buildings tend to be artistically derivative rather than innovative, and in that respect contrast to their antecedents. Regardless, among the most striking are Healy Hall in Washington (1879), the Saint Ignatius Mission Church in Montana (1893), Saint Ignatius Church in New York City (1900), Saint Ignatius Church in San Francisco (1912), Immaculate Conception Church in New Orleans (1930), the Madonna della Strada Chapel in Chicago (1938), and, more recently, the Chapel of Saint Ignatius at Seattle University (1997), Christ the King Jesuit College Preparatory in Chicago (2008), and the Chapel at Jesuit High School in Sacramento (2014).

In the late twentieth century, however, Jesuit artists contributed to launching a musical style that has influenced life "in the pews" to the present, namely, Catholic folk music. At the heart of the story is a group of five scholastics who began composing together at Saint Louis University in the late 1960s and who called themselves the Saint Louis Jesuits. They released their debut studio album (*Neither Silver nor Gold*) in 1974, their best-selling one (*Earthen Vessels*) in 1975, and their most recent one (*Morning Light*) in 2005. The style—characterized by folk-instrumentation, emotive lyrics, and biblical quotations and paraphrases—grew out of a post-Conciliar exuberance for personal expression in worship, vernacular engagement with the liturgy, and easy congregational singing. The style dominated Catholic Church singing in the last quarter of the twentieth century and even found receptive congregations beyond Catholic ones. While the music of the Saint Louis Jesuits is disparaged in some quarters for being "people" music rather than "adoration" music, such hymns as "Be Not Afraid," "Here I am, Lord," and "One Bread, One Body" remain part of the liturgical repertoire in all but the most musically traditional of parishes in the country and are familiar around the world.

By way of comparison, one of their short-term musical instructors, J. Kevin Waters (1933–), represents a different kind of engagement with liturgical music. Waters studied under the serious avant-garde composer Bruno Barolozzi. Long affiliated with Gonzaga University, Waters has prepared new settings for venerable Catholic liturgical texts and prayers such as the *Ave Maria*, the *In dulci jubilo*, and the *Ave verum corpus*, and put to music the religious poetry of William Blake and of Gerard Manley Hopkins (1844–89). He has composed many works for orchestra and small ensembles; his operas include *Dear Ignatius, Dear Isabel* on the friendship of Ignatius Loyola and Isabel Roser, and another, titled *Edith Stein*.

POPULAR CHRISTIANITY AND THE INDIVIDUALLY MISSIONED

A number of Jesuits attained considerable popular reach and national prominence without connection to specific movements and works. Two near contemporaries in the Midwest—John A. Hardon (1914–2000) and John J. Powell (1925–2009)—make for a provoking comparison because of their similar pre-Conciliar training yet contrasting post-Conciliar popularity. On the one hand, Hardon and Powell both earned doctorates in theology from Jesuit schools and, except for the changes affecting Jesuit training in the 1960s as they were finishing their degrees, would likely have spent long careers teaching at the theologate in West Baden Springs, Indiana. After the Council, however, they traveled along more popularizing tracks, each coming to serve and gain the admiration of a different Catholic constituency in the fractious post-Conciliar Church. Hardon's was the more conservative, as he articulated a new anti-Modernist vision for the post-Conciliar Catholic. He worked to revitalize older devotions and practices, Marian and Eucharistic devotions that had by the 1970s fallen out of common use. He founded the Marian Catechist Apostolate (MCA) and the Real Presence Association on the model of pre-Conciliar confraternities. He became a sought-after retreat director and parish lecturer. "The most devastating crisis in the two thousand years of Catholic history is right now," he argued in video classes to the MCA, "and it is mainly the work of the Evil Spirit." He became associated with a range of organizations and media outlets that were critical of the aftereffects of the Council, such as Catholics United for the Faith, *Crisis* magazine, and the cable network EWTN. He published a number of catechetical works, most successfully the *Catholic Catechism* in 1975, which is still in print.

In contrast, Powell, while also publishing widely, gained prominence for his theological openness to psychological insights. His works blended spiritual insight and psychological self-help into what one reviewer called "folksy wisdom" (*Why am I Afraid to Tell You Who I am?*, 1969; *Fully Alive; Fully Human,*

1976; *Happiness Is an Inside Job*, 1989). Sometimes he raised issues of significant social concern, as in *Abortion: The Silent Holocaust* (1981). Powell was early active in video production, and a series of his talks could sometimes be found on commercial television. Late in life allegations of sexual abuse surfaced, which the order acknowledged, casting a pall over his popularizing accomplishments.

In part because of the abundance of early career priests, in part because of a general eagerness to experiment, and in part because of an ambivalence toward established institutions, in the 1970s some Jesuits found themselves assigned to works, sometimes founding them, with no formal connection to the Society. There were many; three examples suffice to give a sense of their variety. One is the work of Richard Thomas (1928–2006). Thomas arrived in El Paso in 1964 to lead Our Lady's Youth Center (OLYC), a center providing employment referrals, banking services, English classes, and social and sports activities for local young people. His experience of life in urban West Texas and on the United States–Mexico frontier and a sustained experience of charismatic renewal led Thomas and some coworkers at the youth center to expand OLYC's mission by acquiring ranch land in 1975. Through the labor of volunteers, both long-term and visiting, the Lord's Ranch, as it was called, became an active farm that supported OLYC's substantial food bank. An associated lay Catholic commune continues to combine for residents—individuals and families—self-sufficient ranch living, a common Christian life shaped by Pentecostal prayer, and apostolic commitment to the local poor on both sides of the border.

Another example is Boys Hope (now Boys Hope / Girls Hope) founded by Paul Sheridan (1943–) in 1977. Starting in Saint Louis, Boys Hope ran residential group homes for children with challenged family backgrounds but who were also scholastically talented and motivated. The residential group homes partnered with Jesuit high schools and provided the residents with the full range of support to sustain a college preparatory education. There are currently homes in fourteen cities in North and Central

America. A third is the Jesuit Institute for Family Life founded in the San Francisco Bay Area by Robert Fabing (1942–). Its aim was to provide Christian marriage and family counseling. Fabing explained his inspiration for the project as coming in the form of a vision in 1961. Founded in 1977, the institute now comprises an international network of twenty affiliates in the United States and eighteen abroad and is staffed by licensed counsellors, both Jesuit and lay.

FAITH AND JUSTICE

The era's spirit of social activism and political engagement shaped the activities of individual Jesuits and the order's commitment to its institutions. Much of the inspiration behind this engagement came from a set of influential documents issued by the general congregations. The single most influential passage along these lines is found in a decree from GC 32, issued in 1975 and titled "Our Mission Today": "The mission of the Society of Jesus today is the service of faith, of which the promotion of justice is an absolute requirement. For reconciliation with God demands the reconciliation of people with one another." These sentiments were a significant driving force behind the developments in Jesuit training discussed earlier in this chapter, as well as behind the new apostolic commitments the order was taking on, the renegotiation of commitments of long standing, and an energized relationship between Jesuits and the laity. Twenty years later, in GC 34, the decree's insight was articulated anew and applied with similar aims in decrees on ecumenism, ecology, and women.

Despite the clarity of vision expressed at the general congregations of this period, on some of the most pressing questions of the day back home, Jesuits could be found on both sides of many barricades dividing the American Church and society. Daniel Berrigan (1921–2016) suffered multiple criminal convictions and incarcerations for his protests against the Vietnam War, opposition to US defense spending, and advocacy for the homeless. The Jesuit parish Christ the King in San Diego joined with the city's

FIGURE 5.3   "Jesuits for Peace," May 1, 1971. Jesuit scholastics join other students from the Graduate Theological Union, Berkeley, California, to participate in San Francisco's May Day peace march in 1971. Source: "Jesuits for Peace," 1971, JARC, California Province Archives, Jesuit School of Theology at Berkeley, box 1, community, buildings, events.

Nonviolent Action organization in the early 1970s to support military personnel who objected to assignment in Southeast Asia. As part of the "Stay Home for Peace" initiative, it provided sanctuary to eleven sailors and pilots who "missed departure" on the aircraft carrier USS *Constellation* in 1971. At the same time, John McLaughlin (1927–2016, left 1975) was writing speeches for President Richard Nixon; and Daniel Lyons (1920–2022, left 1975), a fervent anticommunist and a founder of the reactionary Catholic periodical *Twin Circle*, was denouncing César Chávez, the Delano grape strike, and the US bishops who tried to resolve the strike.

That so many Jesuits worked on campuses drew the Society into the heart of the era's social turmoil. Such turmoil played out in a range of ways on Jesuit campuses. At the College of the Holy Cross, for example, two visionary, albeit personally quite different presidents, Raymond Swords (1918–84, in office 1960–70) and John Brooks (1923–2012, in office 1970–94), moved their institution in progressive directions. Swords endorsed protest against the war and participated in peaceful campus events. When a war-related protest turned into a race-related protest focused on the administration, Brooks, the chairman of the theology department and soon-to-be academic vice president, set out with Swords's encouragement to recruit African American high school students to Holy Cross. Between 1965 and 1969, Black undergraduate enrollment quintupled. Among Brooks's recruits were Clarence Thomas, who later became a Supreme Court justice, and Edward P. Jones, who became a Pulitzer Prize–winning novelist. Calling on students at his final graduation ceremony to "fight for life, for peace, for justice," Swords handed over the reins in 1970 to Brooks, who took a next step in 1972 by enrolling women.

In contrast, at Seattle University positive end results were arrived at by a more tortuous route: The 1968 Tet Offensive radicalized a campus under stress on account of mounting debt and declining enrollment. The scheduled appearance of prowar Senator Barry Goldwater led to vigorous protest and even arson on campus. The university president of five years, Jack Fitterer (1923–2015, left 1978), resigned in 1970 in frustration. His successor, Kenneth Baker (1929–), implemented austere budgetary measures and provoked more student protests. When he resisted the demand of activists to institute a holiday in honor of Martin Luther King Jr., they seized him and plundered his office. The school's lay Board of Regents quickly lost confidence in Baker, who resigned after nine months in office. He went on to become the longest-serving editor-in-chief of the nationally distributed conservative Catholic magazine *Homiletic and Pastoral Review*, newly refinanced in those early years through the efforts of Daniel Lyons. Meanwhile, back on Seattle's campus, Louis Gaffney (1919–94), preaching "contagious optimism," slowly but surely restored peace to the campus, cultivated good relations with the community, and brought fiscal stability to the institution.

MISSIONS AND GLOBAL CONNECTIONS

New forces were at work changing the Church's sense of evangelization and reshaping what US Jesuits were doing in missionary fields. From one side, Church leaders were becoming sensitive to ways that historical evangelization had been fraught with secular colonializing interests and Western cultural imperialism, and so sought forms of mission work more respectful of local cultures. From another side, political challenges were making traditional missions difficult to sustain: processes of decolonization, especially in Africa and Asia, made Western missionaries less welcome; and Cold War tensions manifested themselves in proxy conflicts, especially in Latin America, that demanded new responses from the Church. The effect of these forces on US Jesuit activities in the missions can be captured with reference to developments in three regions: India, Central America, and the domestic missions among Native Americans.

US Jesuits began arriving in India in the early twentieth century. A mission at Patna was assigned to the United States in 1919, and another at Jamshedpur in 1947. Jesuits worked in schools from the primary to the tertiary levels, with special attention to practical training in business and management. But just four years after the India Independence Act, the British *Guardian* newspaper reported in 1951 that "the future of foreign missionaries in secular India is now somewhat gloomy." Patna and Jamshedpur became free-standing provinces, in 1962 and in 1983, respectively. Patna continued the mission started by the Chicago province in Nepal. The proportion of American Jesuits at work in these provinces started declining in the mid-1970s for two reasons: first, the growth of indigenous vocations in those regions; and second, government opposition to the presence of foreign missionaries. As a result of dramatically changing personnel needs and difficulties in maintaining legal residency, many American missionaries in India—Jesuits, along with members of many other religious congregations—began returning home for new assignments and retirement, a transition that was often challenging for those who had expected to end their lives in the missions.

Latin American political independence from European colonial powers had, for the most part, taken place more than a century earlier. In the late twentieth century, Spanish Jesuits were still a significant presence in Latin America. In small numbers, US Jesuits could be found in Belize and Chile. Connections between US Jesuits and their Latin American confreres more commonly developed where they studied together, in houses of formation and graduate programs in the United States and Europe. These connections became increasingly important as the two superpowers began making civil unrest across South and Central America into proxy conflicts and exacerbated economic inequities and social injustices.

While the Church was divided over how to respond, a new theological approach emerged in the 1960s that gave forceful, if also controversial, expression in a Catholic idiom to Latin American aspirations for social justice. Many Jesuit theologians contributed to the advance of liberation theology, as this new approach was called. Due to the international connections of the leading liberation theologians and the networks of communication provided to them thanks to religious orders like the Jesuits, the Dominicans, and the Franciscans, liberation theology was energizing conversations in schools of theology around the globe. The approach provided US Jesuits and their coreligionists across the United States with a new lens through which to view Cold War politics and northward migrations and fostered a new concern that their own country's conflicts with the Soviet Union were impeding the redress of political and economic injustices that Church leaders in Latin America were ever more vocally criticizing.

In the 1980s El Salvador became a focus of attention on account of the US government's support of its regime and a series of egregious acts of violence by that regime against the civilian population. Ever more brazen murders by the Salvadoran military beginning in the late 1970s attracted increasing attention

FIGURE 5.4 Robert Mitchell (1926–2006) helps vest Archbishop Oscar Romero with the hood marking his honorary doctorate from Georgetown University in San Salvador, 1978. At the time, Mitchell was on the board of directors at the university and had recently completed a four-year term as the first president of the Jesuit Conference of the United States. Romero remarked in accepting the award, "This generous gesture . . . has four dimensions that are deeply significant to me, to the Church over which I preside and to its people. First, it is a solid blow struck on behalf of human rights. Second, it is a recognition of all those who labor to preserve and extend human rights. Third, it is an act of solidarity and respect for all those, particularly in El Salvador, who have seen their liberty and dignity trampled upon. Fourth, it is a call to all men and to all nations to heed the Church's plea for human dignity and freedom." A right-wing death squad assassinated Romero in 1980, and the pope canonized him in 2018. Source: Archbishop Romero receiving doctoral hood from Robert Mitchell, 1978, unknown. Reproduced from BFCSC, *Georgetown Today*, March–April 1978.

worldwide. The assassination of six Jesuit priests along with a housekeeper and her daughter at the University of Central America (UCA) in 1989 proved a powerful catalyst to action around the world. In the United States, Charles Currie (1930–2019) emerged as the point man for advocating for US government investigations of the massacre and accompanied many congressional teams to El Salvador. Dean Brackley (1946–2011) was among the Jesuits immediately assigned to take the place of the slain Jesuits at the UCA.

More broadly, Jesuit works became centers of advocacy on behalf of the victimized populations and of protest against the government's support of the military regimes. Jesuits mobilized student bodies and parishes, testified before Congress, and reached out across US society to form coalitions against the militarist terror. The origins of the Ignatian Family Teach-In for Justice were in the School of the Americas Watch, an annual protest begun in 1990 at the gates of Fort Benning in Georgia, where the US Army was training the very Latin American military units behind so many atrocities against civilians. Refugees, plus the increasing, economically inspired migration into the United States, inspired ever greater Jesuit interest in serving the displaced Latin American populations. The Jesuit Refugee Service, whose founding mission was the coordination of international humanitarian aid to the Vietnamese boat people in the late 1970s, worked to similar purpose in the United States along the border with Mexico beginning in the 1980s. The religious needs of the new immigrants led to more Spanish-language training and the introduction of immersion experiences in the Spanish-speaking Americas for Jesuit scholastics. The US and Latin American provinces entered into new "twinning" relationships to facilitate contact and the exchange of resources.

At home, the missions to Native Americans also entered a phase of significant change. A set of influences began converging—internal and external to the order—that compelled the Jesuits to revise how they understood their work with Native peoples. Externally, one can point to the new empowerment movements within Native American communities, including the militant American Indian Movement, founded in 1968. Native advocates were better positioned than ever before to demand an end to forms of social marginalization and cultural suppression that had long been part of white expansionist strategies and that included heavy-handed aspects of Christian catechesis and schooling.

Their activism's influence reached an early high point in the federal government's Indian Self-Determination and Education Assistance Act of 1975, which provided Native American communities on reservations with direct financial grants for social services like primary education and health care that up to that point outside organizations, often churches, had managed for those communities.

Internally, the Jesuits were taking inspiration from Vatican II's admonition to those working in non-Christian societies to approach local cultures and religions with respect and presume goodness and truth in them. An early expression of this newfound sensitivity appears in the decree on "mission service" of GC 31 (1964–65), which insists that Jesuits working in non-Christian communities treat "positive elements of their religions with reverence" as well as their "culture, customs and traditions." A year later, Arrupe drew the attention of US Jesuits to the Native Americans on account of the discrimination and poverty they suffered and against which injustices Jesuits must act. The following congregation (GC 32, 1974–75), which had already linked "the promotion of justice" to "the service of faith" in its fourth decree, posited "inculturation" as an essential aspect of evangelization in its fifth decree. Jesuits were not, the fathers of the Congregation exhorted, to reduce Indigenous peoples to mere objects of conversion but rather to understand them as people alongside of whom they should fight for justice. Addressing a group of Lakotas in 1993, the superior general Peter-Hans Kolvenbach (1928–2016, r. 1983–2008) said, "I am happy that for the past century, members of this Society, the 'Blackrobes,' have walked with you in your struggles. We have desired to be with Christ Crucified in your struggles and to experience with you Christ Risen. I realize that we, as Jesuits, have at times been the source of some of that pain. For that we are deeply sorry."

Finally, in 1995, GC 34 issued a decree—"Our Mission and Culture"—that confessed the order's failure to respect the individuals and cultures it desired to evangelize and thus collaborated in the degradation of "the values, depth, and transcendence of other cultures, which manifest the action of the Spirit." This decree aligned Native Americans with the peoples of Asia, Africa, and Latin America for the first time in a congregational document.

Concretely—and beginning even before 1975—one sees a relationship under strain and in flux. Some ameliorations were symbolic, as when in 1969 the Jesuits renamed one mission from the Pine Ridge Educational Society to the Red Cloud Indian School. Others were more substantial, as when the Jesuits and the tribal government of the Rosebud Reservation negotiated the reassignment of the local school from Jesuit to tribal management in 1974. The same reservation became the site of a series of exchanges, initiated by the Medicine Men Association and Native community organizers, in the mid-1970s. Its aim was to improve the level of respect toward Indigenous religion from non-Native missionary clergy and to shed light on the complex relationship of Indigenous and settler belief systems among Native people. The meetings ended in 1978 without a clear resolution after a contentious discussion of communal values, child rearing, and the role—real and perceived—of medicine men in social and political rivalries. The founding of the Kateri Northwest Ministry Institute in 1989 as a pastoral training program for Native American Catholics developed on the basis of an older tradition of Jesuits' deploying Native catechists to reach places they could not and was also a move away from the clerically controlled mission operation characteristic of earlier generations. Carl Starkloff (1933–2008), at the Toronto School of Theology, and Ray Bucko (1954–), a longtime anthropologist at Creighton University, joined learning and fieldwork in their efforts to understand Native American spirituality and religion. Developments across the last quarter of the century were neither easy nor complete, but they certainly made the Jesuit presence on the reservations different. Some concluded that the developments were signaling the Jesuits' recovery of the principles of inculturation and accommodation that had once made Matteo Ricci (1552–1610) welcome in the Forbidden City and Roberto de Nobili, (1577–1656) welcome at the Mughal court. Others were resigned that after so many

FIGURE 5.5   The sanctuary of the Saint Stephen Mission Church, Wind River Reservation, Wyoming. Johannes Jutz (1838–1924) established the Saint Stephen Mission in 1884 on land offered by the Arapaho chief Black Coal. Jutz later helped establish both the Saint Francis and the Holy Rosary missions in the Dakota Territory. In 1970 the Arapaho artist Raphael Norse began a process of redecorating the church's interior and exterior with designs from Arapaho culture. The baptismal font and altar take the shape of ceremonial drums; and the ambo, a thunderbird. The tabernacle takes the form of a tipi, and tipi poles lift up and support the crucifix. Jesuits administered the mission until 2010, when it was transferred to the Diocese of Cheyenne. Source: Sanctuary of Saint Stephen Mission Church, Wind River Reservation, Wyoming. Alamy Stock Photo / Luc Novovitch, C578M4.

generations of Jesuit-fostered assimilation and government-directed cultural obliteration, it was too little, too late.

Out of the Jesuits' work with Native peoples emerged one of the order's most important and widespread ministries for young adults, the Jesuit Volunteer Corps (JVC). It began as a group of recent college graduates first recruited in 1956 from across the United States to help at a Native Alaskan boarding school founded by the Jesuit bishop of Fairbanks, Francis Gleeson (1895–1983). The volunteer program spread to nearby schools and was eventually organized into the JVC by Jack Morris (1927–2012). The organization spread to the lower forty-eight states, and its ministries expanded. By 2000 the JVC was organized in four additional domestic regions and an international one, and placed about three hundred new volunteers each year in fifty works across eight countries.

The missions to Native Americans in Alaska were also ground zero in the unfolding of the crisis of clerical sexual misconduct for the US Jesuits. The problem did not attain national attention until the first decade of the twenty-first century, when hundreds of legal claims accumulated that alleged assaults by Jesuits and their lay coworkers against Indigenous adults and children on these missions. Some of these accusations were proved in court; Jesuit officials acknowledged more as true or likely. The Oregon province, which had jurisdiction over these missions and others in the Pacific Northwest, ultimately reached a bankruptcy settlement that required $166 million in payment for events spanning the preceding half century. Audits of Jesuit records nationwide have since shown that the calamity of sexual abuse touched all regions and ministries of the Society in the United States and that Jesuit leadership was no more transparent, conscientious, or insightful in handling the problem as it was happening than officials of other orders and the dioceses.

TROUBLESOME JESUITS AND PAPAL INTERVENTION

The ecclesiastical ferment after Vatican II and shifting political allegiances among Catholics stirred up issues that were especially volatile in places where the Jesuits found themselves and that Jesuits felt obliged to address. Among them was the Church's understanding of human sexuality, which the cultural revolution of the 1960s and the promulgation of *Humanae vitae* in 1968 could not have electrified more, and which became an especially blinding flashpoint. In its unfolding, a characteristic Jesuit stance on the matter is hard to identify. A glance at reactions to *Humanae vitae* by three Jesuit contemporaries highlights the complexity. John C.

Ford (1902–89) was among the most esteemed moral theologians of his day. His 1944 essay against "obliteration bombing," for example, is still a touchstone in theological discussions of just war in the modern era. Ford was also among those who, in the deliberations preceding the promulgation of *Humanae vitae*, persuaded Pope Paul VI to reject his advisory committee's majority recommendation to allow married couples certain uses of artificial contraception. Stateside, the urban pastor Horace McKenna (1899–82) was among the priests—the Washington Nineteen—suspended by the capital's cardinal-archbishop for a public statement rejecting the absolute prohibition on artificial contraception within marriage. And in the years that followed, Richard McCormick continued resolutely to distinguish levels of Church teaching in his moral notes and to argue for ways to expand the conditions under which and forms in which married couples could licitly regulate conception.

Two additional cases bearing on the sexual liberation movement also warrant mention. The one has to do with John J. McNeill (1925–2015, left 1987), a theologian trained at Leuven who taught at Fordham and Woodstock in New York. McNeill became a vocal critic of the Church's teaching against homosexual relationships in the 1970s. His work *The Church and the Homosexual* is regarded as the first major piece of scholarship from a Catholic theologian to propose that "homosexual love [is] in itself good love and [can] be holy love." Although the book was published with ecclesiastical permission in 1976, the ensuing controversy led to McNeill's silencing two years later, on orders from the Sacred Congregation for the Doctrine of the Faith, the pope's office for evaluating the orthodoxy of theological positions. McNeill's rejection of a new, expanded order from the Congregation to refrain from any ministry at all to gays and lesbians required his separation from the Society in 1987.

The other case involves Robert Drinan (1920–2007), a law professor and, for a decade, an elected member of Congress (1971–81). He worked throughout his career to defend civil rights in the United States and to expand legal principles of human rights globally. He took up the causes of Jews in the Soviet Union, the racially segregated in South Africa, and the disenfranchised in Central America. After the Supreme Court's decision *Roe v. Wade* in 1973 that limited the state's authority to restrict abortions, Drinan became a proponent of liberalized abortion laws and expanded government funding for abortions. He defended his positions with arguments on the appropriate limits of state action. He argued that the medical community, rather than legislators, had the responsibility for developing appropriate standards. His position on abortion was controversial among Catholics and unsettling within the order. Shortly after his election in 1978, Pope John Paul II required the intervention of Jesuit superiors on the grounds that priests should not hold public office. After being given the choice to leave the House of Representatives or the priesthood, Drinan departed Congress at the end of his fifth term in January 1981. He went on to head Americans for Democratic Action, putting him in an even more political position, in a sense, than the one he left in Congress. In 1996 he wrote in favor of President Bill Clinton's veto of the Partial Birth Abortion Ban. His Jesuit superiors required a retraction, but he continued publicly advocating for even his most controversial positions until his death in 2007.

In August 1981, after Arrupe's resignation as superior general on account of a crippling stroke, John Paul II intervened in the ordinary governance of the Society by placing it under the interim administration of the Italian Jesuit Paolo Dezza (1901–99). The interposition reflected a serious lack of confidence in the order on the part of the pope. Though never officially explained in public except in oblique bureaucratic language, the intervention was likely inspired by controversial actions taken by Jesuits on issues related to the ecclesiastical and civil tumult sketched throughout this chapter. In the ecclesiastical circles of which John Paul II had long been a part, a consensus appears to have emerged that distorted interpretations of Vatican II needed stamping out, that the leadership of the Jesuit order was unsympathetic to this agenda, and that what was done to the Jesuits would pull others in the

Church back into line. While many Jesuits feared the intervention as a prelude to a second suppression, Dezza, with the assistance of another Italian, Giuseppe Pittau (1928–2014), deftly guided this interregnum to a conclusion with the convening of GC 33 in 1983 and the restoration of ordinary governance. The congregation elected the Dutchman Peter-Hans Kolvenbach (1928–2016) as Arrupe's successor on the first ballot. Years of working in Lebanon had honed Kolvenbach's discretion and finesse in volatile situations and made him distinctly suited to restoring the pope's trust in the Society.

Several Americans had significant parts in this episode, foremost among them, Vincent T. O'Keefe (1920–2012), whose removal as vicar general in Rome was the first blow in the intervention. Many Jesuits who lived through the period found the pope's abrupt and distrustful intervention a distressing, even wounding moment in their lives as vowed religious. It bears noting that O'Keefe, deprived of office yet still respected within the order, succeeded in keeping his confreres on an even keel in this stressful and confusing moment. In this respect, US Jesuits did not react differently from Jesuits elsewhere. The absence of reactions that had been anticipated, perhaps even hoped for, in the circles hostile to the Society—such as open revolt against papal authority and exodus from the order on a large scale—demonstrated a miscalculation in the recommendation for an intervention in the first place. In the final analysis, the intervention's significance in the overall history of the Society is arguable. The Jesuits have had troubled relationships with individual popes before, and the order's actual reaction in this case could be taken as an object lesson in its fealty to the papacy.

These instances of unrest in the Church and the Society draw attention to common characterizations of the Jesuits—in the United States and elsewhere—as subversive, rebellious, and refractory. None of these qualities lend themselves to easy measurement. Such generalizations are instead often made by way of comparison between Jesuits of one era and another and rely on a limited number of anecdotes, offered without context. The claims and counterclaims play on historical caricatures of the Society as the Church's light cavalry, on the one side, and a fifth column in it, on the other. Jesuits, from their founding to the present, must take some responsibility for spreading both. The range of Jesuit reactions to Paul VI's encyclical, to offer just one example, speaks against facile generalizations; and cases like those of McNeill and Drinan, as different as they are, point more to uncertain governance in an unstable period than to an organization shifting strategically to one side or the other of emerging American culture wars. In this regard, the Society in the late twentieth century is as much a microcosm or bellwether of the Church in the United States as an agitator within or for it.

Realigning Provinces and Perspectives

In response to the forces shaping the Church and the order in America at the end of the century, the Jesuits entered a phase of intensive national reorganization. They came to this reorganization, one might say, out of both virtue and necessity. The Council itself, after all, had inspired new thinking about priesthood, religious life, and the role of the laity. The Jesuits themselves over the century had developed new ideas about the signal importance of their origins and spirituality, and thus of their mission. Practical matters pressed down as well: beyond the order, the place and contours of America's engagement in religion—for Catholics, as for everyone else—changed dramatically over the four final decades of the twentieth century. Inside the order, it was slowly but surely facing the reality that it had made commitments in the first half of the century that could not be maintained, and some that also should not be.

Apostolic freedom, demographic realism, and administrative efficiency became the implicit watchwords of the reorganization, which lasted nearly thirty years. In 1992 the Jesuit Conference, the order's national office in Washington, released a white paper in the *National Jesuit News* for every Jesuit in the country to inspire "honest and positive" conversation about the demographic changes of the preceding three decades and their implications for Jesuit life and work. The white paper's underlying assumption was that Jesuit service to the Church would be enhanced with greater national vision and cooperation. The white paper was further motivated by a conviction that for any future administrative and institutional realignment to achieve success, individual Jesuits themselves needed to realign the bonds of affection, loyalty, and common cause that united them. The proposals floated in the white paper reflected these concerns: the realignment of provinces, greater collaboration in apostolic sectors at the national level, and more national structures for the governance of the Jesuits themselves. Already a national office, called the Jesuit Conference, had been established in 1972. It was uniquely positioned to help coordinate apostolic decision-making and formational programing across the Assistancy, and it encouraged Jesuit institutions engaged in the same work to develop and meet national standards.

As for the provinces themselves, the original ten were reduced to four. The path this reduction took vaguely reversed the organic expansion of the nineteenth and twentieth centuries, beginning with the reunification of the Chicago and Detroit provinces in 2011. The four provinces of 2020 corresponded roughly to the territorial divisions followed by the European missions two centuries earlier: English and French missions in the east, Italian missions to the west, and the Belgian and French missions of the Mississippi River watershed divided into northern and southern halves.

Regardless of the geographical echoes from the past, the national perspective within those provinces mattered as never before. The extent of a province's geography had less and less to do with decisions regarding training, work assignments, and the maintenance and development of apostolic commitments. The growth and management of major apostolic sectors—pastoral work, spirituality, education, faith and justice, and the like—and formation were handled increasingly at the national rather than

FIGURE 5.6 Map of US Jesuit Provinces, 2020. Source: Jesuit Conference, Washington.

provincial level. In contrast to 1950, in 2000 there was no longer such a Jesuit as one born, admitted, trained, and assigned within the confines of the same one province. There was hardly a single Jesuit work staffed by men of a single province that was not as tightly linked to similar works across the country as to works around the corner or that did not have connections to Jesuit concerns around the globe. The formation of the new Canada and USA Assistancy reflected a continental cooperation for which there was ample precedent. In this respect, the chapter concludes with a mirrored image of what the first chapter offered: at the beginning Jesuits from around the world looked to new possibilities in North America; now Jesuits in the United States, with their brethren in anglophone and francophone Canada, looked at home and around the world for inspiration in how, as Saint Ignatius put it, to best "serve God and help souls."

FURTHER READING

The selected bibliography for this chapter barely scratches the surface of what is available, and the line between primary and secondary literature is porous due to our own proximity to the period.

Primary Literature

Brown, Robert McAfee, and Gustave Weigel. *An American Dialogue: A Protestant Looks at Catholicism and a Catholic Looks at Protestantism.* Garden City, NY: Doubleday, 1960.

Fichter, Joseph. *The Alumni of 1965 Report Back: A Study of 3,722 Alumni of Jesuit High Schools of the Class of 1965.* Washington, DC: Center for Applied Research in the Apostolate, 1974.

Murray, John Courtney. *We Hold These Truths: Catholic Reflections on the American Proposition.* Lanham, MD: Rowan & Littlefield, 2005.

Secondary Literature

Becker, Joseph. *The Re-Formed Jesuits.* 2 vols. San Francisco: Ignatius Press, 1992 and 1997. Becker was the author of an article in *Studies of the Spirituality of Jesuit* that attempted a first evaluation of the demographic decline that first hit the Jesuits in the late 1960s and is mentioned in chapter 5. He became highly critical of changes in Jesuit training that followed the Second Vatican Council and the general congregations of the period. These two volumes are his negative assessment of those changes.

Duminuco, Vincent. *The Jesuit Ratio Studiorum.* New York: Fordham University Press, 2000.

Dunstan, Richard. *A Poor Priest for the Poor: The Life of Father Rick Thomas, SJ*. Vado, NM: Lord's Ranch Press, 2018. The subject of the biography stands at the intersection of two topics highlighted in this chapter: Jesuit involvement in the Catholic Charismatic Renewal, and individual Jesuits' founding works in the 1970s that continue beyond the life of the founders and without Jesuit sponsorship. The biography is well researched and easily read.

Garner, Sandra L. *To Come to a Better Understanding: Medicine Men and Clergy Meetings on the Rosebud Reservation, 1973–1978*. Lincoln: University of Nebraska Press, 2016. The subtitle of this work describes its topic. It is especially insightful at laying out the complexities of the relationships between Native representatives and Jesuits and within the Native communities themselves. This work is valuable in foregrounding Native voices, thus serving as a helpful complement to the account offered by the Jesuit participant William Stolzman (1938–, left 1988).

Lonsdale, David. *Eyes to See, Ears to Hear: An Introduction to Ignatian Spirituality*. Maryknoll, NY: Orbis Books, 2000. Lonsdale offers a helpful sketch of "Ignatian spirituality," as Jesuits have tried to express their spiritual tradition in a modern mode and in a way useful to others besides themselves.

Stolzman, William. *The Pipe and Christ: A Christian-Sioux Dialogue*. Chamberlain, SD: Tipi Press, 1986. Stolzman, who worked many years as a Jesuit on South Dakota reservations, offers a perspective on the possibilities of interfaith understanding between Christian and Lakota religions. Cf. Garner (supra).

Traub, George, editor. *A Jesuit Education Reader: Contemporary Writings*. Chicago: Loyola University Press, 2008. This collection of essays can be read as an attempt by Jesuits to rearticulate their sense of purpose in their educational work. It includes essays by leading educators, most of whom are non-Jesuits reflecting on Jesuit education, and also several governing documents.

Epilogue: A Present between Past and Future

———⊷•⊷———

WE HAVE REACHED A POINT where we must bring this volume to conclusion. Given that the life of the Jesuit order is ongoing, there is no self-evident way to do so. Some of the most eye-catching milestones marking the beginning of the twenty-first century, such as the Thirty-Sixth General Congregation in 2016 and the completed realignment of provinces in 2020, simply do not bring to effective summation the previous four and a half centuries of Jesuit life and labor in upper North America. That must be admitted also for the most eye-catching milestone of them all, the election for the first time in history of a Jesuit as pope in 2013. Strikingly, Pedro Arrupe had appointed Jorge Mario Bergoglio, as a Jesuit priest, to nearly every major office of trust in the Argentine province, from novice master to provincial superior. Then John Paul II named him auxiliary bishop, archbishop of Buenos Aires, and finally cardinal. As archbishop, Bergoglio dedicated himself to the challenges of deep-seated poverty and injustice in his own country in ways resonant with what GC 32, in which he had participated, expressed as "the service of faith, of which the promotion of justice is an absolute requirement." In these respects, Pope Francis's life reflects much of the order's turn-of-the-century spirit, even if not in a specifically North American way.

The eminent mid-century theologian John Courtney Murray may, however, point us toward an exit. Marking the 325th anniversary of Andrew White's landing in Maryland, he declared to his confreres, "To be authentic heirs of our history we cannot simply know and preserve it, but we must move on and enrich it." Murray's remark gets at what makes it so difficult to end this volume: The Jesuits are still adding to their history, and those who do so understand the state of the Church, the Society, and civil society, shaped by what the previous chapter called tumults, not as that which must be lamented in light of the past but as the given, which must be worked in, with, and around, as their predecessors did—sometimes more, sometimes less astutely—amid the "givens" of their day. Accordingly, there is much material worth examining already in the current century, even as historians must wait for time to test it. Nonetheless, an epilogue here may allow for the sketching of some overarching themes drawn from the previous five chapters to serve as benchmarks in a future historical analysis of the present. Nine come to mind, some more obvious than others.

First, the history of the Jesuits and that of Catholicism in America are intimately linked. When the Jesuits arrived in the British colonies, Catholicism arrived, and survived, with them. The Jesuits proved themselves determined, creative, and flexible in meeting the needs and interests of the Church in America. Even once the Church took roots independent from the Society at the Suppression, the Jesuits took a central role after the Restoration in negotiating the relationship between Catholics and American civil society. Jesuits and their many and diverse works have been largely responsible for a Catholicism in the United States that is neither marginalized by outside forces hostile to it nor self-segregating in the manner of a sect. The twenty-first century, secular and religiously indifferent as no other, presents its own challenges, with the threat now more one of subsumation than segregation. How Jesuits and others inspired by their vision negotiate these challenges is a story unfolding.

Second, the Jesuits have a long history of being pulled between serving churched and unchurched populations. "Churched" and "unchurched" are modern terms, of course. Still, with a little imagination, one can see the contours of this distinction across the nearly five centuries covered in this volume. The terms offer a way to evaluate, for example, how the colonial Jesuits negotiated their engagements with settler populations, on one side, and Indigenous peoples, on the other. The distinction can help a comparison of what Jesuit education looked like in 1900 with what it looked like in 2000. Whether in a colonial or modern iteration, the two "tracks" have not been merely rivals for limited Jesuit resources. Works along these tracks have functioned sometimes hand in hand, sometimes complementarily, and sometimes independently. The history would suggest that tension between them has been more synergizing than stymieing. As frustrating as it might be that the US Jesuit history does not reduce itself to one or the other of these threads, imagine the actual history without the one or the other. Mutatis mutandis, the future.

Third, the encouragement, assistance, and collaboration of others have been essential to the success of the Jesuit. Jesuit history is full of "supporting actors" who would be the principals in a more general history and whose kind and variety would be overlooked to the great detriment of fullest understanding of the Jesuits. Thus it is essential to recall the welcome the Jesuits received from the Recollects in Quebec and the Religious of the Sacred Heart in Louisiana, Nerinckx's recruiting of Belgians to Kentucky, and Red Cloud's and Spotted Tail's appeals for schools in the Dakotas. It is also necessary to the history to recall the recurrent collaboration between local bishops and the Jesuits: Georgetown, Saint Louis, Fordham, Xavier—four of their earliest colleges (now each divided into a high school and a university)— were not founded by Jesuits but rather by bishops, clergy, and laity, and only later handed into the care of the Society. Of the two oldest schools they founded on their own and that are still in operation, one was soon abandoned for about two decades because the order could not properly finance it (Gonzaga College High School, 1821), the other was departed from and is an independent Catholic school with a lay board (Saint John's Catholic Prep, Buckeystown, Maryland, 1829).

Sometimes there is an intriguingly ironic dimension to the "help" of others, for example, that it took an Irish-born New York archbishop to get Jesuits long term into New York City, and they were French ones from Kentucky; that Garibaldi and Bismarck were responsible for such a sustained surge in manpower in the United States; and that Jesuits' own demographic decline fostered the development of an Ignatian spirituality, accessible to the laity as never before. In the current moment, there are developments both in the tradition of and beyond these historical precedents. The invigorated Jesuit presence in, say, Atlanta will be fascinating to watch, how it succeeds, and whether it will be replicated: it began with the founding of a retreat house in the mid–twentieth century, but now—in the context of province realignment, with the encouragement of the local archbishop, and in response to the growing Catholic population in Georgia—has been expanded into a mission hub that includes a Cristo Rey school and a parish.

Fourth, Jesuit history is constituted as much by failure as success. The failures themselves and the lessons to be drawn from them are diverse. Many times, the Jesuit responses to failure offer testimony to their flexibility and adaptability. Failure gives us the clearest view of how Jesuits' spirituality shapes their own institutional workings, inasmuch as these workings must be a reaction to it. Thus, Jesuits of the colonial period recalibrated their movements in response to loss: failure in Florida opened up the possibility of success in Havana and Mexico, and the Suppression led to the birth of the national Church and a more vigorous restored order. Other failures are more baleful: the Jesuit participation in American slavery constitutes a calamitous chapter in Jesuit history. This particular aspect of US Jesuit history is especially challenging to understand. On one hand, it shows the Jesuits acting perhaps too "American" in viewing and treating their human property just as the white, propertied class all around them did.

On the other hand, it shows them acting quite "Jesuit," as reliance on slave labor was part of the Jesuit missions in the early Society globally. More recently, Jesuits also showed themselves no more perspicacious than anyone in anticipating or responding to the late-twentieth-century crisis in religious practice. These examples indicate limits, which of course there will be in any human community and institution; the question is how the Jesuits' track record of recoup and recalibration will shape their mission now in the twenty-first century.

Fifth, even for an order famous worldwide as educators, the American Jesuit commitment to education is particularly distinctive. The schools mark the milestones of expanding Jesuit presence in upper North America, beginning with grammar schools in Quebec and Maryland and extending to high schools and universities from coast to coast. The US Jesuits continue to sponsor a large and globally esteemed network of Catholic secondary schools and universities. Although the diminishment over the last half century of Jesuits in the classroom is certainly a challenging loss for their educational mission, Jesuit classicists, historians, literature and language specialists, mathematicians, philosophers, political scientists, and sociologists—all ordained in that same half century—teach, write, and grade innumerable quizzes and papers across their schools. Jesuits administer there, and as chaplains, draw their students more deeply into the challenges and consolations of Christian discipleship. The founding of schools in response to particular exigencies has been a hallmark of Jesuit educational strategy. That continues to the most recent generations and includes not only the new Cristo Rey and Nativity model schools but also new experiments such as Arrupe College in Chicago, founded by Stephen Katsouros (1959–). Arrupe's goal is to offer entry-level postsecondary education to young people from low-income families. As so many Jesuit universities grow in renown for their achievements in research and education and in their service to the national and global Church, Loyola University Chicago, in sponsoring the first Arrupe College, distinguishes itself in this most enduring and fruitful characteristic of the Jesuit educational tradition in the United States: providing educational opportunities to those who would otherwise be left without.

Sixth, the engagement with educational institutions has been complemented by commitment to intellectual accomplishment, especially in the previous century. The Jesuits, more than any other order, and the US Jesuits, more than in any other region within their order, continue to dedicate themselves in numbers to higher degrees and certifications across the full range of sacred and secular disciplines. This commitment has energized all they have done and is among their most substantial contributions to the Church. Newly trained theologians in all subfields, for example, are an exciting presence at the schools of theology in Berkeley, Boston, and Toronto. In secular fields, the sciences are still disciplines where Jesuits make themselves at home. For example, Guy Consolmagno (1952–), a planetary astronomer; David Brown (1967–), an expert in stellar evolution; and Robert Macke (1974–), an expert in meteorites, all make their apostolic home at the Vatican Observatory, and their work has been essential to a sustained and mutually enriching dialogue between science and religion.

Seventh, Jesuits have participated in and fostered public conversations of importance to Catholics, to people of faith, and within the larger American society. The publications of the Woodstock press began that project in the late nineteenth century in serious ways. Radio station WWL, founded at Loyola University in New Orleans in 1922, was an early experiment in that new medium. Daniel Lord made himself a master of religious communication at mid-century through the Sodality of the Blessed Virgin Mary and his many, multifarious, and accessible writings. James J. Martin (1961–) continues the project with his copious writing and high profile in electronic media. Samuel J. Sawyer (1978–), as director of digital strategy at America Media (and newly as editor-in-chief of *America* magazine), works to create platforms for critical conversation and evangelization available to the youngest generation of Jesuits. At the time of this writing, roughly fifty Jesuit scholastics contribute to the *Jesuit Post*, a form

of online outreach to an audience of "young(-ish) adults" and offering "a Jesuit, Catholic perspective on the contemporary world."

Eighth, a commitment to "the promotion of justice" as part
of "the service of faith" is not something US Jesuits simply woke
up to in 1966 but has antecedents going back to colonial times.
The Jesuits negotiated the precarious commitments of secular
governments to religious liberty in the colonial period for the sake
of persecuted Catholic minorities, and they thrived as a result of
its constitutional articulation in the nineteenth century on this
side of the Atlantic. The social apostolate demanded and received
significant Jesuit resources throughout the twentieth century, and
Jesuits proved themselves determined in adapting it according to
the signs of the time in the later twentieth century. To be sure, the
Second Vatican Council and the GCs of the late twentieth century
vitalized this commitment in a new mode. The new models of
schools—Nativity, Cristo Rey, and Arrupe—give evidence to that
ongoing concern—so, too, works like Homeboys Industries in
Los Angeles, the largest gang intervention and rehabilitation program in the world, founded in 1992 by Greg Boyle (1955–); and
the Kino Border Initiative, an advocacy and service organization
for immigrants on the Arizona–Mexico border, founded in 2008
under the direction of Sean Carroll (1966–) and now led by an
alumna of a Jesuit university, Joanna Williams.

Ninth, irrespective of the shifting demographics over the last
five centuries, the Society in the United States has attracted considerable diversity in talent and temperament within its ranks.
Out of this diversity has arisen highly creative achievement, and
thus considerable admiration. At the same time, the fruits of that
diversity have occasioned confusion, frustration, and disagreement in and beyond the order. Attempts to "make sense" of the
Jesuits at this level often resort to caricatures, some old, some
new: "the flyboys of the Church," as the *New York Times* colum-
nist Maureen Dowd put it; "extremists of one sort or another,"
as R. R. Reno declared in an essay in the conservative Christian
journal *First Things*; and "priests with PhDs who protest in the
streets or otherwise advocate for [liberal] causes," in the words

of the *Washington Post* religion reporter Michelle Boorstein. The caricatures, however, beg a question that really matters: how have men as diverse as, to take some late-twentieth-century examples, Michael Buckley, Avery Dulles, Dean Brackley, James V. Schall, Howard Gray, and Joseph Becker along with their many contemporaries, managed—simultaneously to one another, over decades of life, and voluntarily—to stand at the same altar, eat and converse in the same refectory, draw from the same well of sixteenth-century spiritual insights, and assent to the same rule of life. Analyzing the capacity of the Society to be a home for such diversity would seem to be a more productive exercise for coreligionists and fellow citizens alike than the casting of caricatures. Hopefully, the Jesuits themselves do not take their time-tested capacity to sustain diversity for granted either.

As a set, these generalizations reflect, in fact, hopes that have motivated the Jesuits who have labored in upper North America for four and a half centuries. The history is the concretized effort in the United States to strive after what Pope Benedict XVI held up as the universal measure of the Jesuit vocation within the Church: "The Church needs you, relies on you and continues to turn to you with trust, particularly to reach those physical and spiritual places which others do not reach or have difficulty in reaching." Therein, perhaps the two threads—Jesuits working with the "settler" and the "indigenous" populations, with the churched and with the unchurched, with the committed and with the indifferent—most tightly intertwine. How they will be followed into the future is the chapter to be written.

GLOSSARY: WHEN A JESUIT SAYS . . ., IT MEANS . . .

APOSTOLATE. The works that the Society of Jesus sponsors and to which it assigns its members. The term can be applied to a specific work ("the Jesuits accepted that school as an apostolate in 1848"), a general work ("the Jesuits struggled to establish an educational apostolate in the eighteenth-century colonies"), and the general mission of the Society ("the province initiated concerted apostolic planning in 1907"). The word derives from the Greek for "to send forth," which also gives English the very common word "apostle." Also, apostolic.

BROTHER. A member of the Society who is not and will not be ordained a priest. Historically, brothers engaged in manual labor or practiced a trade, and many Jesuit artists and architects in history were brothers. Through formation, brothers, like scholastics, pass through three stages, according to the vows they have taken: novice brothers, until first vows; approved brothers, from first to final vows; and formed brothers (formed temporal coadjutors), with final vows. A Jesuit might also use the term "brother" to refer to any fellow member of the Society.

FORMATION. All aspects of Jesuit training. Formation comprises three major parts: the noviceship, the study of philosophy and theology, and "regency." Two stages of formation distinctive to the Jesuits are regency and tertianship (both infra). A "house of formation" is any Jesuit house in which formation is the designated purpose, thus where the novitiate and tertianship are based, and also where formal study of philosophy and theology in preparation for ordination takes place. This last category may be called a "house of studies," which in turn may be distinguished as a philosophate and theologate, according to what is studied there. Until the late twentieth century, "houses of study" also commonly included a college program (collegiate) and a juniorate, where the humanities could be studied in preparation for philosophy and theology.

GENERAL CONGREGATION (GC). The highest governing body of the Society. It convenes to elect a new superior general or for other extraordinary deliberations. Its delegates come from every province and region of the Society, either by virtue of office (e.g., provincial superiors) or by local election. General Congregations have convened just under once every ten years through history.

MISSION. Like apostolate, a word with several possible meanings. "Mission" could refer to a specific outpost, perhaps consisting of a residence and church; a region in which Jesuits operate that is less self-sufficient than a province and thus has a lower administrative status than a province, on which it might depend; or, in the most general sense, the what and why of Jesuit work.

NOVITIATE. The first two years of Jesuit training, and the place where these two years are based. The training consists of the full, thirty-day spiritual exercises; a set of other brief, intense undertakings called "experiments" (e.g., working in hospitals and begging on pilgrimage); and an introduction to the spirituality, history, mission, and common life of the order. A Jesuit in this phase of formation is called a novice. The novitiate concludes with the novice's taking of first vows of poverty, chastity, and obedience. "Novitiate" can refer to the training that goes on in those two years or to the location designated for this training to take place. "Noviceship" generally refers only to the former. The Jesuit novitiate is unusual in lasting two years, rather than one; in not being preceded by a formal postulancy; and in concluding with first vows that are perpetual, rather than temporary and renewed.

PRESIDENT. See RECTOR (infra).

PROVINCE. A grouping of Jesuits and Jesuit works in a geographic region, designated as such for purposes of governance. The chief administrator is a provincial (superior), whom the superior general appoints for a period usually of six years.

RECTOR. The superior of a larger community. Historically, the title has been used ambiguously, especially in English. It could refer to the superior of a larger, local community of Jesuits, or specifically to a local superior whom the superior general appoints, or also to the director of a school. Historically, at the colleges one man has often exercised both responsibilities over the community of Jesuits and the school itself. The separation of those offices has a complicated history. In this book, for clarity's sake, a Jesuit acting in his capacity as the director of a school has been called a president, even when he would have been called in his own day a rector and even when he was also the local superior.

REGENCY. A scholastic's two- or three-year internship at a Jesuit work, usually separating the periods of philosophical and theological study.

SCHOLASTIC. A Jesuit who anticipates being or is ordained but who has not taken final vows. Through formation, scholastics pass through two stages, according to the vows they have taken: novice scholastic, until first vows; and approved scholastics, from first to final vows, during which time the scholastic will be ordained. Though after ordination, a Jesuit is generally referred to as a "father" rather than a "scholastic" within and beyond the order, he remains a scholastic until he takes final vows. According to the form of final vows a Jesuit takes, his status changes with final vows to either "professed father" or "formed (spiritual) coadjutor."

SEMINARY. An institution for the training of priests. The word is generally associated with diocesan priesthood, not priesthood in religious orders. Jesuit scholastics, for example, are not seminarians.

SUPERIOR. The head of a particular jurisdiction within the order. The actual responsibilities vary according to the level of the jurisdiction in question. In the main, superiors exercise authority over the individuals in their care and oversight over the works in which those Jesuits are engaged. Local superiors usually have jurisdiction over a single community of Jesuits; and regional superiors, over a mission or province. The Constitutions invest a "superior general" with authority over the whole Society. A general congregation elects a superior general to serve for life (with provisions for resignation and removal). The superior general is the only elected superior in the Society; of all Catholic religious orders, the Jesuits are the only ones who elect their superior general for life. The superior general appoints provincial superiors, who hold office commonly for six years. Local superiors are appointed either by the superior general directly or by the regional superior.

TERTIANSHIP. A final year of training for a Jesuit, regarded as the third year of noviceship, but separated from the first two by many years and taking place, in the case of a scholastic, after ordination. Tertianship precedes the taking of final vows.

SELECTED BIBLIOGRAPHY

Studies in the Spirituality of Jesuits. Founded in 1969, *Studies* is a product of the Seminar on Jesuit Spirituality, a group of Jesuits of the Canada and USA Assistancy. The seminar studies topics pertaining to the spiritual doctrine and practice of Jesuits, as well as to contemporary Jesuit life and mission, with special attention paid to the United States. The fruits of these investigations and discussions are published in *Studies*, which currently appears four times per year under the general editorship of Barton T. Geger (1968–):

- *Studies in the Spirituality of Jesuits.* ISSN: 1084-0850. Saint Louis: Seminar on Jesuit Spirituality, 1969–.
- *Studies in the Spirituality of Jesuits* [online]. ISSN: 2328-5575. ejournals.bc.edu/ojs/index.php/jesuit/index.

Woodstock Letters. This in-house Jesuit periodical appeared between 1872 and 1969. Its subtitle suggests its contents: "A Record of Current Events and Historical Notes Connected with the Colleges and Missions of the Society of Jesus." Its focus was on Jesuit activities in the United States. The journal's entries take a wide range of forms, including firsthand accounts, reminiscences, archival reports, descriptive letters, statistical tables, and obituaries. The scholarly pitch of the articles varies accordingly:

- *Woodstock Letters.* 98 volumes. ISSN: 0361-1922. Woodstock, MD: Woodstock College Press, 1872–1969.
- *Woodstock Letters* [online]: jesuitonlinelibrary.bc.edu.

—————

The Jesuits in the United States are always served by being read about in the context of the global activities of the Society of Jesus. Two important general histories of the order—one highly concise, one expansive—provide that global context for this volume:

- O'Malley, John W. *The Jesuits: A History from Ignatius to the Present*. Lanham, MD: Rowman & Littlefield, 2014. A brief review of Jesuit history "from Ignatius to Francis."
- Friedrich, Markus. *The Jesuits: A History*. Translated by John Noël Dillon. Princeton, NJ: Princeton University Press, 2022. A substantial scholarly work by a leading historian of the early modern period that will soon become the standard reference.

—————

Jesuit colleges have been the order's principal institutional and apostolic commitment for the last two centuries in the United States. As such, they have brought Jesuits in sustained contact in these two centuries with more people than any other. The schools thus warrant their own bibliography:

- Rizzi, Michael T. *America's Jesuit Colleges and Universities*. Washington, DC: Catholic University of America Press, 2022. Rizzi's ambitious goal is to tell a comprehensive history of Jesuit colleges from the colonial period to the present. He synthesizes an extraordinary variety of material; and his analysis and judgments are careful, broadminded, and at points prodding. He includes treatment of the several schools that either no longer exist or are no longer affiliated with the Society in addition to those still in operation.

Many schools have sponsored particular histories of themselves. Usually produced in a promotional style for friends and alumni, these volumes tend to offer a rich sense of Jesuits working in local circumstances. Four are singled out here for the high level of their scholarship and their sophistication at highlighting the national, and sometimes international, implications of the local, institutional histories:

- Curran, R. Emmett. *A History of Georgetown University.* 3 vols. Washington, DC: Georgetown University Press, 2010.
- Kuzniewski, Anthony J. *Thy Honored Name: A History of the College of the Holy Cross, 1843–1994.* Washington, DC: Catholic University of America Press, 1999.
- O'Toole, James M. *Ever to Excel: A History of Boston College.* Chestnut Hill, MA: Institute of Jesuit Sources, 2022.
- Shelley, Thomas J. *Fordham: A History of the Jesuit University of New York, 1841–2003.* New York: Fordham University Press, 2016.

Kendall, Daniel, and Gerald O'Collins. *Jesuits, Theology, and the American Catholic Church.* Mahwah, NJ: Paulist Press, 2020. With Vatican II as its Archimedean point, this book is an intellectual history of Catholic theology in the United States. It highlights the sustained contribution of US Jesuits across the principal theological subfields, such as dogmatics, moral theology, and biblical studies.

McGreevy, John T. *American Jesuits and the World: How an Embattled Religious Order Made Modern Catholicism Global.* Princeton, NJ: Princeton University Press, 2016. An introduction to the order's presence in the United States since the Suppression is followed by six case studies drawn from the nineteenth and twentieth centuries. The later chapters focus on how Jesuits in the United States negotiated the tension between being American and being in an order that itself negotiated a tension between the global ambitions of its work and central Roman direction.

Roberts, Kyle B., and Stephen R. Schloesser, eds. *Crossings and Dwellings: Restored Jesuits, Women Religious, American Experience, 1814–2014.* Leiden: Brill, 2017. A collection of eighteen scholarly chapters, this volume takes as its overarching theme the influence of nineteenth- and twentieth-century migration on how Jesuits shaped their institutions of pastoral care, evangelization, and education. It is especially helpful in illuminating a Jesuit worldview in this period that is richer and more complicated than the antiliberal and ultramontane one that is conventionally presented.

Schroth, Raymond A. *The American Jesuits: A History*. New York: New York University Press, 2007. Schroth (1933–2020) offers a history of the Society in the United States in 300 pages, with many incisive and colorful biographical sketches and especially thoughtful reflections on the periods through which he lived.

INDEX

A note on the indexing of schools: Over time, schools sometimes changed names and were separated into high schools and universities. For simplicity's sake, the index entries generally follow the designation (geographical or saintly) of the lower school as it currently exists. Historical names and the names of divided upper and lower schools are included as subentries. For example, what now exists as John Carroll University is indexed under "Saint Ignatius (OH schools)" along with Saint Ignatius High School in Cleveland, and what once existed as Saint John's College in the Bronx is indexed under "Fordham (NY schools)" along with subentries for Fordham Preparatory School and Fordham University.

ABOUT THE AUTHOR

David J. Collins, SJ, has been a member of the Jesuit order since 1987 and is a history professor at Georgetown University. He chaired the university's Working Group on Slavery, Memory, and Reconciliation in 2015–16. He was an elected delegate from the Maryland Province to the Jesuits' Thirty-Sixth General Congregation, which assembled in 2016 to choose the thirtieth successor to Saint Ignatius Loyola as the order's superior general. For more than twenty-five years he has been offering lectures, seminars, and tours to school and Church groups on the history of early Catholicism and the Jesuits in the United States.